Philippe Karl

The Art of Riding

Classical Dressage to High School

Odin at Saumur

Copyright © 2009 by Cadmos Verlag, Schwarzenbek
Copyright of this edition © 2010 by Cadmos Books, Great Britain
Design and Layout: Ravenstein + Partner, Verden, Germany
Photos: Alain Laurioux, Gerhard Kapitzke, Dominique Cullieret, Wulf Rohwedder
Illustrations: Philippe Karl
Translation: Derek Clark (www.holisticequitation.co.uk)
Editorial: Ilka Flegel, Christopher Long
Printed by: Westermann Druck, Zwickau, Germany
Original edition: Une certaine idée du dressage – Odin à Saumur, by Philippe Karl,
© Éditions Belin 2008

All rights reserved. No part of this book may be reprinted or reproduced or utilised in any form or by any electronic, mechanical, or other means, now known or hereafter invented, including photocopying and recording, or in any information storage or retrieval system, without permission in writing from the publisher.

British Library Cataloguing in Publication Data
A catalogue record of this book is available from the British Library.

Printed in Germany
ISBN 978-3-86127-974-7

www.cadmos.co.uk

Contents

Foreword 8

'Hippo-thesis' 11

Why an Iberian
horse? 15

The requirements
of balance 19
    Collection: establishing the
    unstable balance 20
    Collection and conformation 22

Arrival in Saumur 25

Natural asymmetry 29
    Causes 29
    Signs 29
    Effects on locomotion 29
    Consequences for training 31
    Gymnastic development 32
    Characteristics of the basic
    gaits in training 40

Pioneers
of Tradition 43

Work on the lunge 49
    Aids 49
    Gymnastic development 53
    Introducing long reins 53

The jester 57

Philosophy
of academic
equitation 63
    Language of the aids 64
    The seat 65
    The rein aids 66
    Leg aids 75
    The effet d'ensemble 78
    Final considerations 79

Achilles' stallion 83

Lateral suppling
exercises 87
    Work on a single track 88
    Work on two tracks 90

Galas and guest
performances of
the Cadre Noir 97

Exercises for longitudinal
flexibility 101
    Transitions 101
    Simple transitions 102
    More advanced transitions 103
    Rein-back 104
    High School transitions 105

A horse in the media 109

Work at the canter 113
    Canter departs 113
    Counter-canter 115
    Flying changes 116
    Changes in series 121
    Odin 122

The death of Monsieur
de Saint-Vual 125

Collection 129
    Definition 129
    The piaffe 130
    The passage 137
    The pesade 140

Canter pirouettes 145
    Preparing for canter pirouettes 146
    Development of pirouettes 147

Encounters 149

The Spanish walk 153
    Preparation 155
    Jambettes 155

The future 159

To Odin ...

'There is in art, a kind of joy so high
and so exquisite that one is forever indebted
to the one who gave it to you'
Sacha Guitry

For all those who love him.

Foreword

On the publication of this new edition of 'The Art of Riding' it seems to me to be necessary to provide some explanations for attentive and critical readers – the ones who are dearest to me!

The first edition of this book appeared in 1999 in France under the title 'Une certaine idée du dressage, Odin à Saumur', published by Crépin Leblond. The first German edition, 'Reitkunst', followed in 2000, published by BLV.

While 'The Twisted Truths of Modern Dressage' (published by Cadmos) reflects the current state of my equestrian thinking, research and practice, 'The Art of Riding' corresponds to the convictions that I held in the 1990s – 15 to 20 years ago.

The attentive reader will, therefore, be struck by two points in 'The Art of Riding' which reflect the immature views I held at the time of writing. The dogmas of official modern riding have deep roots, and one does not free oneself from them easily.

• Uniform bending of the horse's body
Detailed study of anatomy, movement mechanics and balance of the horse later showed me that uniform bending of the whole horse's body is unrealistic, and furthermore that this mistaken concept tempts the rider by consequence to use his aids in damaging ways.

• Use of auxiliary reins on the lunge
Although at that time I had already dispensed with auxiliary reins when working my horses, the power of the 'dressage rituals' led me to show Odin on the lunge with running reins and in a pesade with side reins. I experienced over and over again, however, that a horse already correctly trained lost some légèreté (lightness) after short sessions on the lunge with side reins, even when they were attached quite freely. This persuaded me to fundamentally reject auxiliary reins except in a special situation in which they represent the lesser evil – in lessons with beginner riders. Even then, they must only be used with extreme care.

It seemed to me sensible to emphasise this development of my thinking over the years; as G. de Levis writes: 'Time wears away the mistakes and polishes the truth.'

Philippe Karl, April 2009

'Hippo-thesis'

In 1934, the Master Armand Charpentier said in one of his talks before the Paris riding club, L'Étrier, that,

'... Xenophon's teachings are so accurate and correct that even after all these centuries (more than twenty three) there is nothing more to add ... The parade horse described by the conqueror of Scillonte could have been ridden by Cazeau de Nestier and the suppling of the neck by the relaxation of the mouth could have been written by Baucher.'
(André Monteilhet, Les maîtres de l'œuvre équestre)

Accordingly, it would appear that there can be nothing more to invent in equitation, so it may seem presumptuous and futile to continue to write about this distinguished art. Must many years' comprehensive experience therefore be simply dismissed?

Wisdom rightly states that 'experience is a lantern carried on one's back that illuminates only the path already trodden'. At least the pathfinder gains the satisfaction of illuminating the road for those who follow him, and this is exactly the mission of every teacher who takes his calling seriously in all its greatness and transience.

Perhaps out of cautious reserve, there are many gifted écuyers* who have left nothing behind, and one could say they 'hid their light under a bushel'. A pity!

As for the rest, their modesty sometimes serves only as a virtuous mask for intellectual sluggishness, or as a comfortable alibi for dubious competence.

No one can expect absolute certainty and infallibility from a teacher. He is entitled, nevertheless, to lend expression to his convictions if he says what he does and does what he says. He who is congruent in word and deed demonstrates a sincerity that should earn him the right to a few mistakes, and at least some goodwill, if not respect. The competence of an écuyer lies in a constant search for perfection in four areas.

Knowledge

'Theory is the knowledge, practice the ability. Knowledge should always take precedence over action.'
(Alois Podhajsky, The complete training of the horse and rider)

Horsemanship is part of a nation's cultural heritage, and France is one of the most richly endowed. However, many riders take too literally what General L'Hotte overstated:

'One does not learn the art from books because they inform only those who already know.'

This results in an often crazy empiricism dressed up now and then with the feathers of snobbery. This trend has its own language – coded, numerical, based on purchase prices, profits, average values, indices, breeding lines, orders, computer lists – a technical jargon that relates more to 'business' than culture, and cannot pretend to replace it.

Neglecting the experience of our predecessors means one fails to put one's own practice in perspective, and impoverishes it by robbing it of technical and historical references. In addition one must admit that, without becoming overly scientific, any useful conception of equitation incorporates a knowledge of anatomy, physiology, the science of locomotion, animal psychology, etc. Finally, our knowledge develops thanks to our nicest virtue,

---

*Écuyer is often translated as instructor or riding master; however, this does not fully reflect the particular meaning and gravitas of the term in France. An official rank at Saumur, écuyer implies someone who trains horses and good riders, and it is awarded only to those with long-standing practical experience in all aspects of riding, a comprehensive appreciation and understanding of riding culture and an extensive specialist knowledge of the horse.

curiosity itself. Every rider's observations are instructive if they give rise to an objective, unprejudiced analysis.

Of course, education is not the same as competence, and no écuyer can be the pure product of his library. That would require a belief in some kind of 'spontaneous generation'. Reading, observation, reflection, study of the theory and practice mutually enhance one another.

'Above all one must ride a lot, without letting the books gather dust on the shelves.' *(Nuno Oliveira)*

Expertise

'In riding, science and art are often wrongly opposed to one another. There, practical know-how, the domain of the artisan and art, the aesthetic object, domain of the artist, come together. But only in High School and sometimes in sport can riding evoke the sentiments of beauty, which is the domain of art.' *(Jean Licart, Équitation raisonnée)*

At this level, riding becomes a form of expression at least as demanding as dance or music. It is not always the most gifted riders who go furthest, since precisely because they find it so easy, they may become dilettante. One could say that is their 'Achilles' heel', as described in the song of Georges Brassens:

**'He had the gift, that's true,
I admit, he was a genius,
but without technique, a gift is
nothing more than a bad habit ... '**

Only daily, stubborn, often thankless, almost ascetic practice can produce real mastery. Although the professional must remain an amateur in the etymological sense of the word, one who does it out of love, it is not possible to produce excellent performance by being amateurish in any discipline.

Hence, certain artists' circles should be regarded with caution. They mostly consist of followers of the 'vaguely brilliant', and castigate with more pretension than competence the 'laborious sticklers for principles'. The latter are at least honest workers. Art can only exist with enough virtuosity to free oneself from material compulsions. This requires flawless technique.

Everyone knows that the dance is found between the movements, that music springs from between the notes and that poetry originates between the lines ... but at the price of untiring work that enables one to avoid missteps, dissonances and errors in spelling, grammar or syntax.

To the extent that classical horsemanship strives, like the art of dancing, for the 'difficult ease' from which the beauty of the movement arises, the rider may profit from meditating on the verses of Claude Nougaro:

**'The dance is this cage,
in which one learns to fly'**

Passing it on

Without an appreciation of equestrian culture and without competence in the education of horses, teaching is not possible. Riding has the specific feature that the teacher must also be the manufacturer of his educational tools. Besides, we are dealing with a sentient being, where every intervention constitutes an act of training, for better or for worse.

'Riding and training cannot be separated. By the simple act of sitting on a horse, one is unconsciously training or de-training.' *(Gustave Le Bon, L'Équitation actuelle et ses principes)*

The teacher sharpens the horse if he works it, and the pupil dulls it if he uses it for his education. If the lessons are given prudently, the rider acquires a feel for the 'edge' of the horse without blunting it. Put simply, the écuyer must frequently take back his work, even re-make it.

It is evident that one should be careful not to confuse lessons with educational theory. By way of provocation, seasoned instructors sometimes say with irony: 'what you can't do, teach ... if you don't succeed at teaching, specialise in educational theory'.

Educational theory offers possibilities to improve the transfer of knowledge. Concerned with diverse teaching styles and methods, it is absolutely worthy of interest, but one must beware of underestimating the importance of the message itself. After all: 'What do I care about the bottle, so long as I get drunk?'

Of course, the all too frequently heard 'watch me ... and do the same' is especially unsatisfactory. A good instructor has wisdom born of experience, and is moderately extrovert and a benevolent disciplinarian, clearly: the generosity one calls a 'gift for teaching'. To the teacher, this is like the musician's ear and the dancer's feel for rhythm. These talents are innate – one can always work on them and refine them, but never create them.

Making oneself understood

An écuyer in the true sense, someone who applies solid equestrian knowledge and experience to the education of his horses and is keen to pass on what he has learned to others, can only agree with the following definition:

'Equitation, in reality a scientific art, is the more or less skilful application of different sciences. Reducing as much as possible the component of skill in it is the only possible way to advance it and to give riders (while appealing to their intellect) lessons that do not remain superficial ...' *(Gustave Le Bon, L'Équitation actuelle et ses principes)*

Thus in any comprehensive conception of horsemanship, any technique which does not lead to a logical result, which cannot be shown to be part of a method which itself conforms to academic principles, should be rejected as a common trick. This speaks to the intellectual rigour of the rider and his honesty as an instructor – to his credibility.

In the light of his experiences, the écuyer's knowledge and skills must ensure that his theories become ever more comprehensive, yet more convincing and simpler. He will be interested in educational theory only insofar as he must adapt the exercise to the training of his horse, adjusting his language and his explanations to the age and the intellectual abilities of his pupil.

An instructor who is content to teach only 'what to do' produces, at best, trained monkeys on machines. One who tries, however, to teach an understanding of what one does, how, when, why and for what purpose, produces riders deserving of the title, even if of only modest abilities.

The art of riding consists above all of learning to understand the horse: how to use him without abusing him. In this sense it brings out the 'man of honour', justifying Wachter's masterly definition:

'The art of riding can be summarised in two words: fairness and correctness.' *(In French: justice et justesse.)*

Through this subtle guidance the pupil becomes truly independent, and the teacher is the opposite of a guru:

'A good master knows how to make himself superfluous.' *(René Bacharach, Réponses équestres)*

It is clear that aspiring to the title of écuyer means embarking on a constant search for a level of perfection which everyone knows is not to be found on earth. It is said: 'One is not an écuyer, one is always becoming one.'

So now, after more than thirty years of enthusiastic practice and passionate apprenticeship on that long road to Rome by way of Saumur, it is time to take stock.

The horse is the raison d'être of the rider and the écuyer's calling card. It is only right that Odin and his training should be the subject as well as the guiding thread of this account, sometimes technical, sometimes anecdotal. Several reasons justify this choice:
• He was the first horse in my career that I could train all by myself for more than three years from the time when he was started.
• His repertoire is extremely broad: work on two tracks, flying changes, tempi-changes, canter pirouettes, piaffe and pirouettes in piaffe, passage including half-pass at passage, pesade, Spanish walk, work on long reins and in-hand.
• He came with me to Saumur in 1985 and took part in gala performances of the Cadre Noir in France and abroad from 1986. For 12 years he was one of the main attractions of these events as a soloist under saddle and on long reins.
• As an occasional schoolmaster he was a 'stepping stone' for a whole string of instructors and advanced amateurs.
• His life story is at the same time atypical and eclectic. Atypical, because he was the first Lusitano stallion accepted by the National School of Equitation – which did not happen by itself. Eclectic, because he appeared in many unusual and sometimes astonishing surroundings: arenas, circus, theatrical stage, TV studio – even in dressage competitions!

In the end, I dare to hope that I may be forgiven for the title of this preface which, while indeed something of a play on words, at least conveys the exact intention of this work:

It is the thesis of a keen student; a horse is the advocate of this cause.

Although this is the fruit of long-standing research, nevertheless, it remains a hypothesis that can only be refined yet further in the future.

'Every horseman with long-standing experience can make certain comments which were not signposted by his predecessors or which eluded them, because the knowledge and use of the horse represents an inexhaustible field of investigation and observation.' *(Alexis L'Hotte, Questions équestres)*

One should not take these words of encouragement from General L'Hotte too lightly because, as several anecdotes attest, he was not known for being overly generous with them. So, it is with the gratitude and respect that his work and memory deserve that I would like to dedicate to him these few 'memoirs of a civilian écuyer'.

Why an Iberian horse?

Sometimes one is fortunate not to have things too easy. Coming from a riding family, I might no doubt have inherited an exclusive taste for a certain discipline, and for this type or that breed of horse. That, however, was not the case. On the contrary, I was forbidden from riding until I had reached an age when I could work and pay for it myself. On the day that I decided to make it my profession and give up my medical studies, it was time to pack my bags. It was a matter of a well-reasoned, even if not so reasonable choice, of a personal aspiration, deeply and very dearly held. A long-standing frustration and my awareness of the handicap of such a late beginning meant that my zeal and my curiosity knew no bounds. Very quickly I found myself more attracted to the writings of La Guérinière and Parrocel's engravings, than competition results and pictures of dressage horses. An inexplicable question of taste! Thus I found out in the course of my reading that the Iberian was 'the horse of kings and the king of horses', the most prized in all the academies of Europe from the Italian Renaissance up to the end of the eighteenth century.

Confronted with this voraciousness, and with tastes close to his own, my first riding instructor, M. Portelette, had the excellent idea to entrust me with Nuno Oliveira's book: 'Réflexions sur l'Art Équestre', and then the happy inspiration to take me to his friend, M. Henriquet. I was immediately seduced. I discovered horses and a style of riding which imposed themselves upon me with the strength of an aesthetic ideal, summarised in one word: roundness – which is also, by the way, the hallmark of good jumping!

From then on, I could not help but be interested equally in jumping and the art of riding. That allowed me to experience for myself how the greatest contrasts in my subject could be resolved: the Andalusian fans considered me a daredevil because I jumped with pleasure, while the competition dressage riders thought me a crazy exotic because I did not scorn Iberian horses or even Lipizzaners ... not yet an écuyer, but already a collector!

Certainly, a few engravings from La Guérinière, or showing Monsieur de Nestier riding Le Florido, nestling between a Louis XV armchair and a Louis XVI chest of drawers place many a rider 'in the right company', but his taste for antiques will not always stretch to training a descendant of these horses.

• To some these are not 'proper' horses. So logically they would have to eat their words if a rider succeeded in achieving genuine and comprehensive results with one. In their defence, it has to be said that all too often one sees mediocre presentations or caricatures of this breed, with would-be riders who abuse their generosity, take themselves for educated masters and, of course, cannot condemn the rest of the equestrian world harshly enough.

• To others, these horses are so easy that there is no merit in training them. Thus it should be dishonourable to work with such aptitude, but commendable to acquire a 'talented' German horse with gold! Should one shun a talent for collection if one has ambitions toward High School? I cannot think of anyone who would keep a four-year-old for jumping if he runs under the poles, or try to win at Auteuil with a Percheron!

If one considers modern dressage in the context of the history of equitation, one discovers very quickly that what is held up today as representing the 'everlasting values' is perhaps just current fashion. Some examples:

• The extended trot, so highly valued at present, was regarded by the old masters as a vulgar gait, appropriate only for coach-horses. To go fast, nature gave us the canter, a point of view that speaks for itself.

• Also, out of simple common sense, the flying lead change was regarded not as an air, but only as a banal movement serving an utilitarian purpose. And when in the middle of the nineteenth century François Baucher launched his changes of lead at every stride (tempi-changes), while it was the height of popularity in the circus, the supporters of academic equitation regarded this tour de force as a tasteless quirk.

• On the other hand, airs like the pesade have fallen into oblivion. Is there, however, a better proof of the mastery of collection?

Let us live in our time, because we must, but consciously and without disavowing our equestrian inheritance either from arrogance or from ignorance.

Why a stallion?

One is first tempted to answer: because they are born that way if nature did not make them mares.

Then again, I was also from the beginning in an environment where it was, as far as possible, normal to leave stallions entire irrespective of their breed. Of course, there are also exceptions. A few horses turn out to be dangerous and must be castrated, but they are a small minority. The majority, however, do not belong in everybody's hands, because of the need for a deeper obedience, crafted by an experienced rider.

So it was understood that the cavalry in general could not keep entire horses that would be ridden in ranks with arms and packs by riders of modest ability. After that, out of force of habit and an inclination towards ease and comfort, this practice became systematic.

Fortunately, for several years the best dressage and jumping riders have been turning up at competitions with stallions.

It is without doubt because of waiting too long in selecting stallions for the character traits associated with aptitude under saddle that French breeding, so genetically rich and so successful in jumping has, nevertheless, not succeeded in producing good dressage horses and must submit today to the dominance of German horses in this discipline.

Without getting too philosophical about it, it is a little hypocritical to proclaim 'the nobility of man's most virtuous conquest' and 'the manly virtues of equitation', when the systematic removal of the body parts which contribute to the horse's fire and pride is a discourteous precondition.

In pragmatic terms, it goes without saying one would rather ride a quality gelding than an emotionally disturbed stallion, and a good Selle Français than a mediocre Iberian.

In summary, let's say that no breed is perfect (that we know) and that all are worthy of study and respect, whether equine or human!

Discovery and purchase

Odin was acquired by M. and Mme. Huré in September 1983. Mme. Huré had at that time been a keen riding pupil of mine for six years, and owned a horse which was not registered but was hot enough to be christened 'Fogo' ('fire' in Portuguese). I had broken him in for them; Fogo was an excellent teaching horse, but he was getting on, and it was time to begin looking for a successor. They wanted my help in finding a pure-bred Lusitano whose education they would entrust to me.

Several of my pupils had already bought horses from M. Roger Bouzin, whose excellent stud was in Rethel in the Ardennes, so we agreed to meet at his private riding stables in Le Havre to try out two horses.

M. Bouzin, a lawyer, passionate breeder and rider, a straightforward and charming man, welcomed us – M. and Mme. Huré, my wife and myself – with the hospitality for which he is renowned.

The first candidate was four and a half years old, big and attractive-looking. He had been started and already looked a very pleasant horse in all three basic gaits.

The second candidate was three and a half but his conformation was questionable in three important areas:

• He was croup-high and built downhill. Since horses of this breed are generally built uphill and mature only at the relatively late age of approximately six years, one could still hope to see his withers rise. But it was not guaranteed.

• He stood over himself in front and narrow to the base.

• On the other hand, he stood very wide at the hocks.

His gaits were more appealing. A good, long walk. a very expressive, elastic trot, although his canter was modest – a little short and with an inclination to rush. Under saddle he went like a barely started three-year-old, swaying under the burden of the rider's weight. Two main impressions stood out: a great sensitivity, and more suppleness than strength.

A detailed examination of conformation and gaits favoured the first horse. But the second displayed a mixture of grace and majesty that reflected a very strong personality.

'His Highness' certainly lived up to his name: Odin. It was indeed as if the Norse god of war himself had walked into the arena as if into a territory just conquered. There was already something of the dominant stallion in his manner. His papers went a long way to explain these qualities, because they mentioned three significant Portuguese stallions: MV – Manuel Veiga, RA – Ruy de Andrade and CN – Coudelaria Nacional.

I was still weighing the pros and cons when Mme. Huré and my wife, both inspired by the charm of this 'Monsieur', overcame my remaining reservations with their enthusiasm. Cold, scientific, equestrian considerations gave way to a certain je ne sais

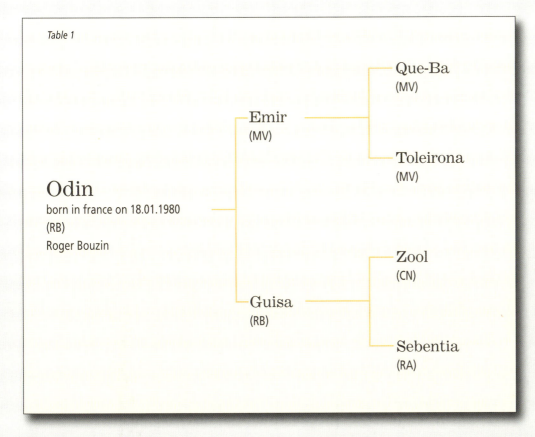

Table 1

Odin
born in france on 18.01.1980
(RB)
Roger Bouzin

Emir (MV)
— Que-Ba (MV)
— Toleirona (MV)

Guisa (RB)
— Zool (CN)
— Sebentia (RA)

quoi. One doesn't have to look like Apollo to be a dancing star! The decision was sealed there and then.

The first exchanges

Odin had hardly arrived at my stables before he took possession, trumpeted, strutted around and let everyone know that he was ready to deal with any objections. He was kind towards people, but hot-blooded and aggressive with his stable-mates. Even today, it is still out of the question to allow him direct contact with a neighbour, and his rider must keep him absolutely on the aids if another horse comes within a range of 10 metres or less. He requires constant vigilance. In similar vein, horses passing by his box must often make a detour to keep themselves out of range of his teeth. He is very serious about his territory!

In the first months, his owner spent a lot of time on him and got him ready for riding. He began to take advantage of her maternal spirit. To avoid being bridled he first stretched his nose skywards then, later, reared. Tightening the girth disturbed him considerably and he tried to bite. Eventually I had to intervene with some paternal authority – saddling and bridling him on a line, and scolding him audibly at the slightest hint of any undesirable behaviour. He began to understand that there were two bosses in the yard, and that I was not the more accommodating. With all horses, but even more so with stallions who show a strong sense of their own will, one must never forget that they appreciate only those whom they respect. Firmness when required; gentleness as much as possible. And one must not confuse firmness with brutality, or gentleness with vapidity. The horse is to the rider what the sound box is to the strings of the guitar ... it amplifies everything, including the bum notes! Don't they say, 'Let me ride your horse and I will tell you who you are'?

Before work, Odin was always loosened up on the lunge, and sometimes with a lesson on long reins. Under saddle, some precautions were necessary in the first months. In effect, he was not yet submissive enough for me to ride him in the presence of other horses. Indoors or outdoors, but always alone. All well and good; however he was extremely distracted and called endlessly to the others. In the riding hall he even reared now and then, to look over the wall and spy the horses whose presence he had sensed. In a loud voice I let him know what I thought of that ... while simultaneously using an exaggerated opening rein, the leg on the same side and a tap with the stick to oblige him to return to the ground. Very soon he contented himself just with shouting ... annoying, but safe.

The requirements of balance

The experiments conducted by General Morris and Baucher, and later confirmed by Captain de Saint-Phalle, showed that all horses are built 'on the shoulders'. The forelegs of a horse standing freely on all four legs carry an average of one-ninth more of the total weight than the hind legs.

The presence of a rider sitting in a neutral position increases the imbalance yet further, since two-thirds of his weight are also carried by the forelegs.

The natural balance of a horse is, therefore, on the forehand. Its polygon of support is long and narrow, and the centre of gravity is a long way toward the front. The forces of the hind legs are entirely for propulsion. This configuration is very favourable for speed. If the rider stands completely in the stirrups, the forehand carries over four-fifths of his weight. Thus the purpose of the posting trot, the 'two-point' seat and the jockey's position becomes self-evident.

Fig. 1

① *Elongated base of support: the preferred balance for speed*
② *Unstable balance: mobility in all directions, subject to balance and impulsion*

The most manoeuvrable horse, and therefore the best trained, is, however, the one who can mobilise himself instantaneously in any direction with such economy of effort that the interventions of the rider remain invisible. This can only be achieved by putting the whole ensemble in an 'unstable balance': only under these conditions can a substantial mass (that of the horse) be easily influenced in all directions by a much smaller mass (that of the rider) which is superimposed upon it.

In his Étude des corps superposés ('Study of superimposed bodies'), Charles Raabe made this remarkable comparison: 'The juggler who places a peacock's feather vertically on his nose continually adjusts his base of support to keep the feather in balance. By its movements, therefore, the feather causes the juggler who supports it to move around.'

This is the fundamental challenge of equitation: to establish the 'unstable balance' that enables effortless mobility, to abandon it and return to it at will. That defines, in simple terms, the equestrian concept of collection.

Table 2: Overloading of the forehand

Free-standing horse

1/9 of 540 kg = 60 kg
1/3 of 75 kg   = 25 kg
Total   = 85 kg

With elevation of the head and neck plus flexion at the poll

85 kg – 1/25 of 540 kg = 63 kg

The improvement obtained is appreciable, but still not nearly sufficient.

Collection: establishing the unstable balance

1. Elevation of the neck and flexion at the poll

As the experiments conducted by General Morris with the help of Baucher show: allowing the head and neck to fully extend, or elevating them as much as possible, transfers approximately 1/25 of the horse's total weight towards the front or the rear. The meaning for a horse weighing 540kg, mounted by a rider weighing 75kg, is outlined in Table 2.

2. Engagement of the hind legs

When the hind legs step far enough under the body, they carry more of the load and thereby relieve the forehand. The polygon of support shortens from the rear, and the centre of gravity falls in the middle. In this way the relatively unstable balance is achieved.

3. Standing over in front

If at the same time the horse's forelegs slant behind the vertical, the horse shortens his base of support from the front. The polygon of support is shorter, but the horse has more of the load on his shoulders. This is incorrect.

'Goat on a mountain top'

At the price of extreme engagement of the hind legs, a balanced distribution of the weight can be restored. This posture, the so-called 'goat on a mountain top' which characterised Baucher's first manner, is therefore questionable. In effect, instead of generating mobility it blocks the horse:

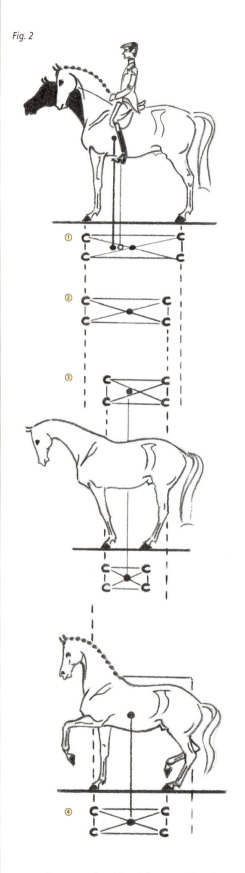

Fig. 2

Base of support and position of the centre of gravity
① Free-standing horse, with and without elevation of the neck and flexion at the poll
② With hind legs engaged under the mass
③ Horse simultaneously standing over his front legs
④ In a correct piaffe

• The convulsive engagement of the hind legs opens all the joints and therefore kills any chance of developing propulsion, because only a compressed spring can extend.

• Because of their sloping position under the body, the forelegs can only move with difficulty. The range of movement of the shoulders is restricted.

• At the same time, the point of the shoulder moves back and leads to overflexion of the neck, which in turn causes the horse's nose to come behind the vertical. A dangerous invitation to the horse to come behind the bit!

The only interesting aspect of this posture lies in the extreme flexion of the lumbar spine that it requires. But this should be rejected, since the disadvantages far outweigh the advantages.

4. True collection

True collection is, therefore, this equestrian 'state of grace' which allows unstable balance to be connected to activity. The ideal becomes reality in the piaffe:

• Vertical alignment of the foreleg in the support phase.

• Elevation of the base of the neck

• Flexion at the poll, whereby the nose stays slightly in front of the vertical

• Active lowering of the haunches through increased flexion of all joints, from the lumbar spine to the fetlock and including the hock and stifle

• The horse grows taller and the forehand becomes lighter, so long as the hindquarters continue to push the mass upward.

Collection and conformation

There are certainly some aspects of conformation that make it easier to realise this unstable balance which characterises collection. Let's now investigate Odin's strengths and weaknesses.

1. Proportion

Most desirable is the 'square' horse, with the line from the point of the shoulder to the ischia the same length as the height to the withers. Odin falls into this category. It is self-evident that a rectangular horse has a longer polygon of support which moves it away from the unstable balance.

2. Top line

The withers and croup should lie on the same horizontal line. If the withers are higher, the horse is built 'uphill', which can be of some advantage. Odin, in contrast, is built 'downhill': height at the withers; 1.60m, height at the croup; 1.65m. The loins and back slope downwards towards the front, something that tends to put him on his forehand.

3. Alignment of the forelegs

The ideal alignment of the foreleg is that it stands as an absolutely vertical supporting pillar. Odin, in contrast, stands a little over his forelegs. This defect often accompanies and magnifies the effect of a plunging top line. It is a definite handicap.

4. Neck

Recalling the famous weight measurements mentioned above, General L'Hotte reminds us: 'The same investigations have shown us that a long, although light, neck loads the shoulders more than one that is thick but short ... this is because the long neck is attached lower down.' It follows, then, that the ideal neck must be attached high with a strong base, somewhat short and becoming finer towards the head. It should form an angle of about 45 degrees with the trunk. One may say that such a horse has 'a good neck'. Odin corresponds to this definition, except that the top of his neck lacks a little fineness.

5. Head

Located at the end of the long lever formed by the neck, a lighter head brings less weight onto the forehand. As is often the case with this breed, Odin has a somewhat heavy head with very strong jowls. This is not advantageous, even though he is very expressive.

6. Attachment of the head

If the parotid gland lies in a distinctive channel, the attachment of the head will be well disposed to flexion at the poll. In Odin's case this area is somewhat thick which, in combination with his heavy jowls, makes flexion at the poll more difficult.

7. The back

As the weight-bearing region, the back must be straight and strong. If it is weak or saggy the back will hollow under the rider: the horse will elongate his base of support and the weight will come on the forehand. The lumbar spine, principal area of power transmission and hinge between the hindquarters and trunk, must be absolutely powerful and supple at the same time. A short lumbar area is strong but often stiff, while a long lumbar region is supple but often weak. The ideal lies in between. Fortunately, Odin is equipped with this advantage. So, although he stands over in front and is a little 'downhill', his back and lumbar area are good.

8. Haunches

The haunches are the seat of activity, the 'motor' of the horse. Hence, they must be long, well-formed and strong. With the Iberian breeds one often finds horses with dominating shoulders and a short croup: a defect with which Odin, fortunately, is not afflicted.

9. Alignment of the hind legs

Odin is 'placed': the back of his cannon-bone lies on the vertical line dropped from the point of the buttocks. Well-formed joints and strongly developed hocks favour active engagement of the hindquarters under the mass. Viewed from behind, he stands very wide at the hocks which leads, unfortunately, to his hind legs splaying in collection.

10. Shoulders

Because Odin is built croup-high and stands over in front, his shoulders are also short and upright. These characteristics taken together serve only to limit the range of motion of his forelegs. Just as a very sloping shoulder combined with short cannons favours the long, low stride of the racehorse, a steeper shoulder combined with longer cannons creates a 'high knee-lifter', that is to say, a tendency for greater flexion and elevation of the foreleg, just as in collection. Odin falls into the latter category. The ideal would be a horse who shows as much length in his stride as he does elevation.

Fig. 3

Above: the ideal 'square horse'
Below: Odin

Arrival in Saumur

In September 1984, the magazine Plaisirs Équestres published an article with the heading 'Striving for complete gymnastic training of the riding horse'. My preface began with the words: 'I am often asked: Are you most interested in dressage or in jumping? My habitual answer: Neither one nor the other ... just horse riding! Must one resign oneself to the alternative: the sometimes frenzied pragmatism of the "jump rider" or the often self-serving, sad formalism of the "dressage devotee"? Is it not possible to combine respect for the traditional values of classical equitation with a modern practical purpose such as show jumping? Moreover, is there no possibility of a method that allows the renunciation of makeshift solutions like castration and the systematic use of auxiliary reins?'

Over ten pages, this article described the education of an Anglo-Arab stallion. His name was Jobard and he displayed an inclination to difficult and violent behaviour that led his owner, R. Gommé, one of my former pupils, to entrust him to me. My article was illustrated with twenty photographs which showed the horse working on two tracks, in the piaffe and the Spanish walk, as well as jumping large fences.

A few weeks after the article was published my telephone rang.

It was Colonel Durand, Écuyer en chef of the Cadre Noir. He had read my article with great interest and would like to meet me. Would I be willing to give a short lecture to the student-instructors of the National School of Equitation?

'It would be a great pleasure, Colonel, and an honour for me!', I responded – eventually, but not before considering for a moment how I could unmask the perpetrator of this little joke!

Although I had every reason to be surprised, there was actually no reason for suspicion. Colonel Durand, appointed as Écuyer en chef of the Cadre Noir after a brilliant career as an international showjumper, could very well be interested in my dream of syncretism – especially as this was also his own hobby-horse.

An appointment was duly agreed, and after our meeting he suggested to me that I join the School within a few months, as soon as a post became free. Reflection, hope, waiting ... then it came to be that Colonel Durand, himself only recently appointed as director of the School, recruited me for a four-month trial period from 1 April 1985. I cannot express deeply enough my gratitude to him for this invaluable opportunity.

Since he couldn't give me any school horses immediately, Colonel Durand suggested that I should start my service with some private horses. Thus I arrived with two Selles Français that went into jump training – and with Odin who was entrusted to me by his owner, because she found him too strong and difficult to manage by herself. By this act M. and Mme. Huré demonstrated a trust and a generosity for which I will be forever grateful.

These four months of probation were not a comfortable time. Inspite of the benevolent care of the manager and the courteous attention of the Écuyer en chef, Colonel de Beauregard, I felt like a 'foreign body' in this 'organism'. I was anxious

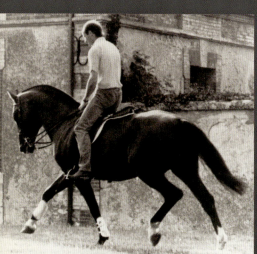

Jobard in 1984

that the 'graft' should take, rather than be rejected. Observe, learn and adapt while still being myself: a delicate game, played for high stakes!

A few very close friends had not failed to point out to me that it might look quite flippant or even provocative to arrive in Saumur with a Lusitano in my luggage. My answers to their concerns were:
• 'Nuno Oliveira was given an official welcome there several years ago …'
• 'Until proven otherwise, the School is looking for riding instructors, not diplomats …'
• 'Out of loyalty, dignity and friendship, I will not abandon this horse.'

At the School, Odin didn't exactly help us blend in unnoticed. Grey, but not quite the colour of the walls! In spite of all precautions he sounded off at every opportunity. It seemed to me as if he was the only one I ever heard. So much for discretion!

Fortunately for me, the Écuyer en chef had nothing against stallions. As it happened, he himself rode at that time a marvellous Anglo-Arab stallion called Béryl, whom he owned. He was an excellent horse who, however, couldn't care less about his stable-mates. Colonel de Beauregard understood me, therefore, and I had his sympathy for my horse's loud and untiring impressions of Don Juan and Caruso.

As for the rest, their reactions to my horse ranged from mildly astonished sympathy, to the most perfect indifference, tainted with a little contempt.

At the end of a fateful four months Colonel Durand confirmed my appointment and outlined my future at the institute:
'There comes a time when one must specialise. I know how difficult the choice is, because I have experienced it myself, but you must give up jumping. The School needs instructors, and your development will have to lead to your acceptance into the Cadre Noir.'
'Of course, I understand.'
'Concerning your grey, I cannot promise you that you can keep him at the School.'
'I'll think it over, Colonel.'

Thus, he invited me with as much tact as determination to decide for myself something that he did not want to force upon me. Slowly, the door of the School was closing on Odin. I was

Odin, shoulder-in left in trot

disconsolate, of course, but also firmly resolved to keep a foot in this door, by whatever means. Apparently, however, the God of émigré horses and obstinate riders intervened, because suddenly an unexpected opportunity came up. A riding instructors' course was planning a final celebration with presentations in the big riding hall of the Cadre Noir and asked me whether I could do 'something'. We were in this situation together and we had a free hand!

Odin's first performance

Although already well advanced in his education, Odin was not yet six years old. He was still very excitable and had no experience of public appearances – never mind under floodlights. It was playing with fire, but 'who dares, wins!'

I decided I would make use of the sociable, student atmosphere of the evening to avoid the stereotypical rituals of dressage. Out of personal taste as well as for reasons of stylistic coherence, I decided I would present Odin to the music of Mozart, accompanied by me in a Louis XV costume cobbled together from whatever I could find.

On the appointed evening he delivered a more than honourable performance, consisting of lateral work in all three paces, passage, piaffe – and more than a few resounding whinnies!

As I rode out of the arena with relief and recognition, I dedicated to Odin these words of Cid, another tormented Iberian:

**'I am young, it is true, but in a noble soul,
Virtue doesn't depend on the number of years.'**
(Pierre Corneille)

This presentation brought me some compliments, combined with a suggestion: 'You are interested in classical horsemanship, your horse seems promising and corresponds to the taste of the old masters. Would you agree to test out the possibility of creating a historical presentation?'

This unexpected offer came from an instructor who, because of his very particular tastes and a significant equestrian and musical education, was attempting to enrich and diversify the Cadre Noir's performances – and all with the approval of the Écuyer en chef. His name was Alain Francqueville, and I am delighted to record my appreciation for him here. Without his open-mindedness, the persuasive power of his ideas and his friendly support, Odin would have a much harder time, as would I. Needless to say, I accepted the offer with enthusiasm.

Natural asymmetry

There are plenty of scientific treatises about the locomotion of the horse; I can't recommend highly enough the excellent work, Équitation raisonnée ('Rational Equitation') by Commandant Licart. By examining the interaction between natural asymmetry and the motion sequence, we will find the core of all training problems.

'Just like every person, every horse comes into this world with two unequal sides, one strong, the other weak.' *(Jean Licart, Équitation raisonnée)*

Causes

The position of the embryo in the womb has the biggest influence on the horse's natural asymmetry, because the foal lies rolled up with his or her neck over the body to one side or the other. Accordingly, one would expect foals to be born 'left-handed' or 'right-handed'.

Traditionally, one stands on the left side of the horse at all possible opportunities: in order to lead, bridle, saddle, girth, mount, groom etc, so that the horse, one might say, ends up adopting a bend to the left. One cannot deny that this plays a role, but what should one think of the horses which remain bent to the right in spite of all this? Besides, this cause is easy to eliminate if one only takes care to do everything from the right as much as the left. The horse's education can only benefit.

Signs

The mane falls to the hollow side – unless it has been deliberately brushed to the other side! Odin's mane fell originally to the left. When he was a four-year-old, it had to be shaved, to clear up a bad summer skin infection. This 'short back and sides' stood him in good stead, even more so in Saumur, so it stayed until he was more than fifteen years old. When it finally grew back, the mane fell again by itself to the left. How stubborn nature is!

A horse that is bent to the left makes itself hollow on the left side; in other words, it holds its head to the left and falls on the right shoulder. This is the case with Odin. Such a horse also frequently stands when free with his left lateral pair of legs closer together. Here also, Odin is no exception.

These signs reveal the natural bend of a horse quite well. Especially if one perceives contradictory signs while riding which are due to incorrect work.

Effects on locomotion

Most studies have shown that locomotion is associated with oscillations of the spine in both horizontal and vertical planes. Put extremely simply, these oscillations appear as follows:
- At the walk and in trot, the symmetrical step sequences produce a succession of 'S' and reverse S curves. In both of these gaits the horizontal oscillations predominate, because the hind legs step alternately under the body.
- At the canter, the horizontal oscillations are significantly reduced. On the left lead they form an 'S', on the right lead a reverse 'S'. On the

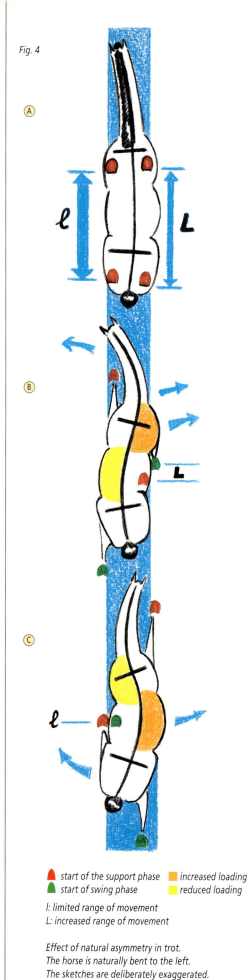

Fig. 4

▲ start of the support phase ■ increased loading
▲ start of swing phase ■ reduced loading

l: limited range of movement
L: increased range of movement

*Effect of natural asymmetry in trot.
The horse is naturally bent to the left.
The sketches are deliberately exaggerated.*

other hand, because at the canter the two hind legs engage and then push almost simultaneously, it is the vertical oscillations of the spine which dominate. The same is true for jumping, bucking or rearing.

Consequences of natural asymmetry in trot

Figure 4 B
• The trot stride is illustrated at the end of the suspension phase: the left diagonal pair supports the mass, the right diagonal pair begins to swing forward. At this moment the spine forms a reverse 'S'.
• The head is carried well to the left causing the base of the neck to shift to the right. This causes a significant overloading of the right shoulder which pulls the horse towards this side.
• The clear left bend of the neck limits the reach of the left shoulder and promotes that of the right shoulder.
• Hindered by the natural asymmetry, the thoraco-lumbar vertebrae bend only a little to the right. Hence, the passive mass (chest and belly) is pushed only a little to the left.
• Associated with the limited dorso-lumbar bending: limited engagement of the right hind leg and restricted push of the left hind leg.

Figure 4 C
• End of the subsequent suspension phase: the right diagonal pair supports the mass, the left pair begins to swing forward. Now the spine forms an 'S'.
• Restricted by the natural asymmetry, the neck bends only a little to the right. The limited movement of the base of the neck leads only to a partial loading of the left shoulder. Thus the shoulders remain displaced to the right.
• This limited right bend does not restrict the reach of the right shoulder (which was promoted previously by the strong left bend). In addition, the neck, which is only slightly bent to the right, pulls the left shoulder only slightly forwards.

• Favoured by the natural asymmetry, the thoraco-lumbar vertebrae bend strongly to the left. Therefore the passive mass is pushed significantly to the right.
• The strong bend of the thoraco-lumbar vertebrae encourages a more pronounced engagement of the left hind leg and a stronger push of the right hind leg. As a result, the hindquarters are displaced to the left.

In summary, natural asymmetry to the left affects the trot, just as it does the walk, as follows:
• Displacement of the shoulders to the right and the hind quarters to the left.
• The right diagonal leg pair reaches further forward than the left.
• The right side is overloaded.
• The left lateral leg pair shortens while the right lateral pair opens.

Effects of natural asymmetry at the canter

Sketches 5A and 5B show the second phase of the canter stride. At this moment the diagonal leg pair has just taken the weight and the horse is supported on three legs. In canter on the right lead, the right foreleg touches the ground next, while in canter on the left lead the situation is reversed.

Right-lead canter
With every canter stride the spine alternates between an S curve and a reverse 'S'. The natural asymmetry tends to increase the left bend of the neck and restrict the right bend of the thoracic and lumbar vertebrae.

The consequences for the forehand include an increased range of movement of the right foreleg at the expense of the left, as well as a clear overload of the right shoulder. The horse also displaces the hindquarters to the right so that the right hind leg can reach further forward than the left in spite of the limited dorsal bend.

Fig. 5

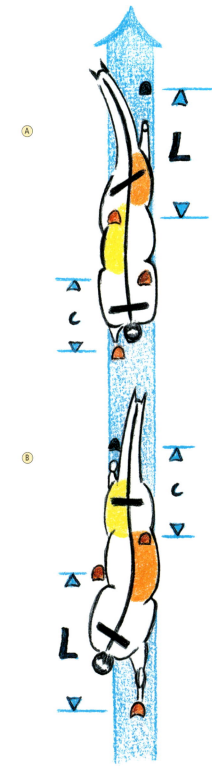

🔺 triangular base of support
⬛ next footfall
l: short base of support
L: long base of support

*The effects of natural asymmetry at the canter
The horse is naturally bent to the left.
The sketches are deliberately exaggerated.*

Natural asymmetry

It follows then that right-lead canter tends to straighten the horse with limited engagement of the right hind leg and modest push of the left hind leg.

Left-lead canter

The picture is reversed. With every canter stride the spine alternates between an S curve and a reverse 'S'. The natural asymmetry to the left will hinder the right bend of the neck and increase the left bend of the thoraco-lumbar vertebrae.

The consequences for the forehand include a restricted range of movement of the left foreleg and also a slight holding back of the right foreleg. Loading of the left shoulder is reduced. For the hindquarters, the effects of the natural bend and the canter mechanism add together.

It follows then that the hindquarters fall out further to the left due to increased engagement of the left hind and the strong push from the right hind leg.

Consequences for training

Overall, natural bend to the left corresponds to an inclination to overload the open right side and to relieve at the same time the closed left side. This has the following consequences for training:
• The left hind leg engages more than it pushes. The right hind leg pushes more than it engages.
• Turns to the left are 'with the balance', with a tendency to enlarge the radius of the curve with the shoulders while the neck over-bends to the left.
• Turns to the right are 'against the balance', with a tendency to fall on the right shoulder and decrease the radius. The neck tends to bend to the left and the hindquarters drift outwards.
• The horse prefers to canter on the left lead but not straight.
• Evasions to the right whereby the horse falls onto the right shoulder with the neck broken to the left.

• Lateral work: the horse prefers to move his shoulders to the right than to the left and his hindquarters to the left than to the right.
• In rein-back, a tendency to drift to the left
• The right diagonal leg pair reaches further forward than the left one: while rising to the trot, the rider will tend to rise with the right diagonal leg pair.

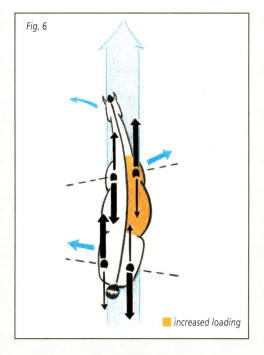

Fig. 6

■ increased loading

The effects of a natural bend to the left

What the rider feels
• More contact in the right rein than the left.
• With each step, the seat drops more to the left than the right.
• Left leg feels longer and more lies closer in (left side concave). Right leg is pushed further off (right side convex).
• Imbalance to the right.

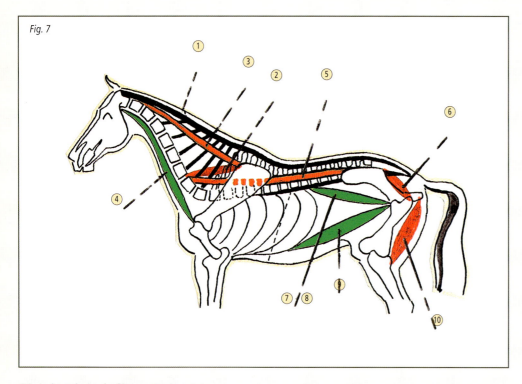

Fig. 7

Principal muscles involved in movement

Gymnastic development

Summary of the muscle groups that play a major role in locomotion:

1. **Nuchal ligament.**
2. **Serratus muscle:** raises the base of the neck.
3. **Splenius:** elevates the neck. Opens the angle between head and neck (extending at the poll).
4. **Brachio-cephalicus:** flexes and lowers the neck. Flexes at the poll (if the 'fixed point' is at the humerus) and/or lifts the point of the shoulder caudally (if the 'fixed point' is at the head).
5. **Longissimus muscles:** elevate the base of the neck. Extend the lumbar spine and sacro-iliac region.
6. **Gluteals:** open the hip joints.
7. **Psoas minor:** flexes the sacro-iliac joint.
8. **Psoas major:** flexes the lumbar spine, the sacro-iliac joint and hip joints.
9. **Abdominals:** flex the lumbar spine and sacro-iliac joint.
10. **Hamstrings:** flex the stifle ('fixed point' at the pelvis). Flex the sacro-iliac ('fixed point' at the shinbone).

Some preliminary remarks

One of the best-known quotes in horsemanship is General L'Hotte's famous maxim: 'calm, forward and straight'. At first sight and when understood as a description of the goals of training, this formula smacks of being a simple truism – but on a deeper analysis, including consideration of the means to be employed, it represents a summary of systematic, progressive gymnastic training.

Calm

Calm, as an expression of state of mind, does not mean apathy or disinterest. Physically, it is characterised by the absence of tension. Here we are concerned not with the rhythmical muscle contractions necessary for movement but rather with persistent and undesirable tensions which affect locomotion and interfere with training. These 'resistances' can be resolved only by 'de-contraction', that is to say, by lengthening of the antagonist muscles:

'If one flexes a joint, it is not the muscles which cause the flexion that one supples but rather those which oppose because they must give way, relax.'
(Alexis L'Hotte)

Calm, therefore, is manifested through flexibility.

Forward

A calm horse can make his forces available to the rider. The full range of his capabilities will only be available, however, if both his hind legs push equally. Since locomotion is associated with oscillations of the spine which increase in amplitude the longer the strides, it follows that the gaits will be limited only by a lack of flexibility. Even everyday language confirms this when we speak of a horse that is 'bending to his task', since to do so he must of course bend and unbend. One can perhaps replace the catchphrase 'no impulsion, no horse' with 'no suppleness, no horsemanship'.

Straight

One can only draw out the horse's full capabilities, not to mention preserve the physical integrity of his body, by the equal and appropriate distribution of loads. This naturally leads us to consider straightness, since in terms of biomechanics the latter can only be the consequence of symmetrical oscillations of the spine about the axis of movement. Of course, this is also a question of suppleness. It is perhaps interesting to note that the term 'dressage', despite it's rather daunting and authoritarian connotations, originally meant 'to set straight'.

To overcome the consequences of natural asymmetry one attempts to make the horse 'ambidextrous'. This represents a task without end, about which d'Auvergne says:

Natural asymmetry

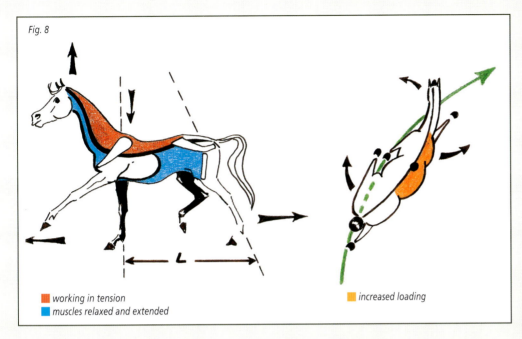

Spontaneous reaction of the untrained horse to the rider's weight and tension of the reins.

■ working in tension
■ muscles relaxed and extended
■ increased loading

'The horseman, with all the perfection of his art, spends his life trying to correct this imperfection.'

In conclusion: since one can only collect a horse that is 'calm, forward and straight', one must first develop his lateral flexibility to obtain, in the end, the longitudinal flexibility which itself characterises collection.

Definition
From straightening to collection or from lateral suppleness to longitudinal flexibility.

Statement
The young horse reacts spontaneously under saddle to the disturbance caused by the rider's weight and the presence of the bridle by contracting all the muscles of his top line … and therefore, all the muscles of the lower line let go. The consequences include: lifting of the head, opening at the poll, pigeon throat, sinking of the withers between the shoulders, hollowing of the thoracic and lumbar spine, disengagement of the pelvis and hind legs, elongation of the base of support. These are all conditions which favour speed and long, flat strides.

On a circle, the same horse turns by a loss of balance, is bent to the outside and falls into the turn on the open, inside lateral leg pair. The hindquarters skid outwards, the horse falls on the inside shoulder and uses his neck as a counterbalance. The whole horse is in a crooked position and is light years away from collection.

For reasons of didactic clarity the progression suggested below includes only the major exercises and is divided into three separate steps. In reality, of course, the phases can more or less overlap.

I Introduction: Relaxation of the top line, Forwards in natural balance

Why?
By contracting, the brachio-cephalicus muscles can only flex the poll and round the neck if the splenius muscle lengthens. Then the cervical part of the serratus muscle raises the base of the neck in conjunction with the nuchal ligament whose tension rounds the whole spine.

The contraction of the psoas and abdominal muscles can only flex the loins and engage the hind legs under the mass by the amount that the longissimus muscle stretches. Since this stretch of the top line is conceivable only while moving forward in a

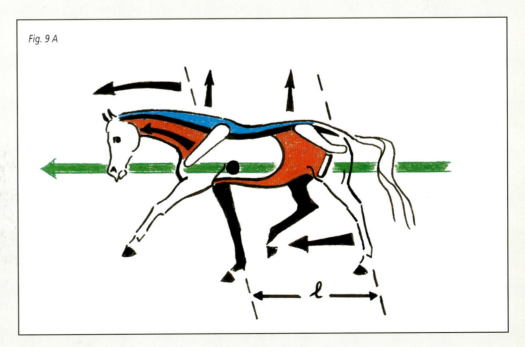

Correct neck extension

natural balance, it is by the extension of the neck that the horse can be ridden at the same time 'on the hand and in front of the legs'.

'Whether one is breaking-in or retraining a horse, one must always begin with stretching exercises.'
(Jean Licart)

How?

Under the pretext of stretching the top line, one may naturally be tempted to exaggerate the flexion at the poll until the horse's face comes strongly behind the perpendicular. This overflexed posture (in French: encapuchonée) offers infinitely more disadvantages than advantages.

Advantages:
- One can quickly achieve an elementary form of domination, most often through the incorrect use of auxiliary reins. A comfortable palliative.

Disadvantages:
- What the rider believes to be légèreté (lightness) is only a retreat 'behind the bit'... from where the horse can then take the initiative.
- Because the horse does not establish a correct relationship with the rider's hands, the latter can be deluded into thinking his horse is in balance when he is really on the forehand.
- The convulsive contraction of the brachio-cephalicus muscles completely blocks the free movement of the shoulders.

Overall there is a danger that the horse who is strongly on the forehand and limited in his forward movement loses his sharpness, falls behind the rider's legs and becomes, perhaps, even restive.

Definition

When stretching well, the horse lowers his head and stretches his neck away from the withers, until it is roughly horizontal; the cervical vertebral column loses its natural, S-shaped bend, becoming nearly straight. Visually, the goal is achieved when the underline of the neck becomes straight. The horse extends his neck, pushing his poll over his mouth as a prolongation of a lengthening, rounding back.

Naturally the degree to which the head lowers depends on conformation. A deeply set 'ewe neck' can be corrected only by a deeper position which can be lower than the horizontal. By contrast a higher, more majestic, maybe even ideally attached neck requires a stretch that only approaches the horizontal. In both cases, however, the stretch of the neck is essential, even if for opposite reasons. It is at the same time a necessary duty and a warranty for the future!

By what means?

How can one achieve the relaxation of the top line which, if it is shortened and hollow, opposes flexion at the poll and, ultimately, collection?

Extension of the neck

Inversion of the neck (ewe neck) is caused by the simultaneous contraction of the right and left splenius muscles. Lateral bending of the neck whereby the splenius muscle on the convex side stretches is sufficient to correct

Fig. 9 C

Muscles working in tension
Stretched muscles
Increased loading

Straightening the horse via bending and thereby stretching the muscles on the outside

this faulty posture. The inversion of the neck is anatomically incompatible with a pronounced lateral bend.

When necessary, the rider can make use of this reciprocal relationship: bend causes stretching – stretching increases flexibility.

Thus, by frequent changes between right bend and left bend the resistance is dissolved and, in the end, the horse rounds the neck and lowers the head: 'If the fruit is ripe, it falls from the tree.'

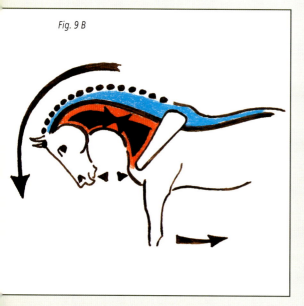

Fig. 9 B

Overflexion of the neck

Stretching of the dorso-lumbar-sacral region

As with the neck, the incompatibility of hollowing and lateral bend also applies to the dorsal and lumbar regions of the spine. Since the longissimus muscles also connect the pelvis to the base of the neck, it follows that a clear bend of the neck pulls the front insertion of the back muscles on the convex side forwards. This explains why the bend of the neck spreads 'by infection' to the rest of the spine.

With the help of the bend the horse can adjust his whole backbone to the curved line on which he moves. Thus the harmony is restored: the bend holds back the inside shoulder and promotes the reach of the outside one which has to cover more ground. The hind leg on the convex side pushes more than it engages; while the leg on the concave side engages more than it pushes.

Furthermore, the lateral bend of the neck pushes its base toward the outside shoulder and the lateral bend of the dorsal and lumbar spine shifts the passive mass towards the outside. The horse adjusts himself to become 'straight on the curve' and carries himself. Instead of falling into the curve he turns 'in balance'.

He no longer uses his neck as a counterbalance, rather the rider uses it to 'steer'.

Yielding the hindquarters

On a circle, if the horse's haunches move to the outside so that its hooves trace three tracks, this encourages engagement of the inside hind foot under the mass while at the same time developing the flexibility of the dorsal and lumbar regions. Since the hind legs describe a bigger circle than the forelegs, they take larger steps. The rider can increase the action of the hind legs, therefore, without acceleration of the gait and without compromising the natural balance. By progressively tightening the circle, this practice leads eventually to the pure turn on the forehand.

Uses

• A useful means of addressing especially sluggish haunches.

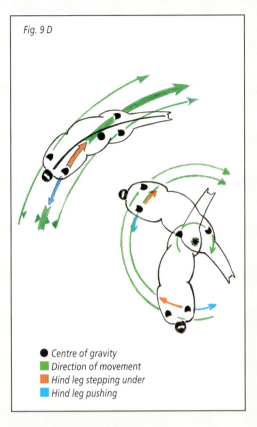

Fig. 9 D

● Centre of gravity
■ Direction of movement (green)
■ Hind leg stepping under (orange)
■ Hind leg pushing (blue)

Yielding of the quarters in shoulder-in position leading to turn on the forehand

• While turning around the inside foreleg the horse must almost totally relieve the hind legs and overload the forehand – something he can do only by stretching. Thus this method presents an effective means of 'forcing' the stretching of the neck.
• Furthermore, this gymnastic procedure is a non-violent and intelligent way to disarm the first signs of rearing. In effect, it takes away the horse's leverage point for the resistance and he remains squarely on the shoulders.

Limits

This practice is interesting only as a means of correction. Prolonged and systematic use is not justified from a gymnastic point of view because, the smaller the circle becomes, the more the hind legs must cross and the less the inside hind engages forward under the mass. Eventually the horse goes completely on the forehand, without any forward movement, a state with severe undesirable consequences.

The old masters taught their horses to yield their quarters with the aid of a single pillar. (Seville Arena)

II Confirmation: Development of flexibility and mobility in all directions by work on two tracks

Taking possession of the hindquarters

After initial correction of the natural bend by adjusting the forehand on curves on both reins it is time to establish more precise control of the hindquarters to enable the perfection of straightness. The rider reaches this second level with the help of lateral exercises on two tracks which make the movements of the hindquarters more harmonious and stronger.

Basically there are only two kinds of lateral movements:
- either the horse moves in the direction of his concave side; in 'travers' position;
- or he goes in the direction of his convex side; in 'shoulder-in' position

Choice of method

With which to begin? It's a very old debate. La Guérinière's descendants answer: with the shoulder-in. And Baucher's sons state: with travers – even going so far as to reject the former.

If we give the horse 'the casting vote', as it were, two observations help us form a commonsense, unprejudiced opinion.

If a horse shies to one side of his own accord he always bends the neck in the opposite direction to the movement – whether it is to duck out before jumping a fence, to elude an aggressive herd member in the pasture, to escape the attack of the bull in the arena, or just to get away from some frightening object! This would tend to speak in favour of the shoulder-in.

If the horse's shoulders are steered in a certain direction, the hindquarters, in contrast, move in the opposite direction. One must only lunge a horse in an energetic trot on a small circle or work it in-hand to observe this effect, which L'Hotte describes exactly in Questions équestres. One more argument in favour of the shoulder-in.

In conclusion

Now, as we know, successful education must progress from the simple to the difficult and because of that one cannot start by contradicting nature. Clearly, therefore, lateral work must begin with the shoulder-in.

Thus the famous saying is confirmed: 'Let him think he is his own master and he will more surely be your servant.'

Shoulder-in

Definition

While bent to one side, the horse moves towards his convex side. His hooves trace three tracks on the ground with the outside diagonal leg pair and his centre of gravity lying on the axis of motion.

Advantages

As we have seen during our investigation of the motion sequence, the lateral bend of the spine has two natural consequences: the advancement of the outside diagonal leg pair and the displacement of the hindquarters to the inside. The shoulder-in permits the extinction of the latter effect by clever exploitation of the former. In effect, the shoulder-in develops the range of motion of the outside diagonal leg pair as the inside hind leg steps obliquely under the body (the 'outside' diagonal comprising the outside fore and inside hind leg with respect to the bend of the horse). This is, therefore, a key exercise in the development of straightness.

The tracks of the front hooves lie quite close together. The horse must clearly cross his forelegs which improves the freedom of his shoulders.

Supported by the lateral bend, the inside hind leg engages further forward and under in the direction of the centre of gravity which implies a significant flexion of all joints with lowering and increased loading of the inside haunch. Consequently, the shoulder-in balances the horse toward the inside hind leg which must in turn provide all the propulsion. The exercise supples and strengthens at the same time.

Limits

If the angle of the shoulder-in is exaggerated, it can reach the point where the horse can no longer cross his knees. Then the inside hind leg is no longer in a position where it can push the body, something which restricts the forwards movement. The greater the crossing, the less the engagement: this leads to a loss of balance, the horse falls sideways and hollows his back. A distortion which proves that 'more' is not necessarily better.

In principle, one could say that the shoulder-in makes it possible to collect the horse one half at a time by suppling and straightening in the direction of motion. By definition, it produces an active shortening of the outside diagonal leg pair, in other words, a diagonalisation of the gait in question. It was very perceptive of Gustav Steinbrecht to refer to the shoulder-in as the 'trot posture'.

Though it may upset the 'fundamentalist' followers of Baucher (who quote with pleasure the unfortunate joke: 'Shoulder-in, an excellent thing … I never use it!') – this movement remains a fundamental exercise. In fact, how can one doubt an exercise that is as natural as it is effective in every way (suppleness, straightness, balance) and so useful as to be considered 'the first and last lesson to be given to a riding horse' (La Guérinière)?

Travers (half-pass)

Definition

The horse is still bent, but now moves in the direction of his concave side. This time he aligns the inside diagonal leg pair and centre of gravity with his axis of motion. The travers is the logical continuation, extension and the precise opposite of the shoulder-in.

Advantages and limits

The travers develops the range of motion of the inside diagonal leg pair – the leg pair which is held back and disadvantaged by the natural bend. Because the hoof tracks of the forelegs lie further apart, for the same angle of

Natural asymmetry

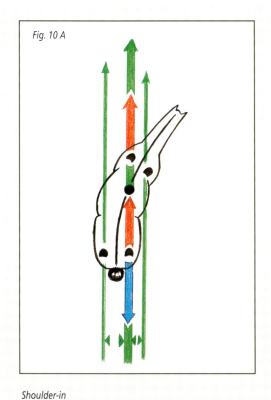

Fig. 10 A

Fig. 10 B

Shoulder-in

Travers and half-pass

displacement the horse crosses the forelegs less than in the shoulder-in.

Lying on the convex side, the outside hind leg is in a position where it can push better than it can reach under the mass. Because the hoof tracks of the hind legs lie quite close together, the degree of crossing increases to the detriment of engagement. While the shoulder-in improves the bend and generates collection, both are pre-requisite for a correctly executed half-pass. The hind leg on the concave side which is actually ideally placed for engagement cannot, in fact, do so because it must move sideways with every step. This is why one so often sees a poorly executed half-pass with the haunches leading.

Left shoulder-in at the trot

Half-pass to the left at the trot

37

Interaction: gaits – lateral work

The mechanism of the canter, with the specific feature that one lateral leg pair reaches ahead of the other, facilitates lateral steps. For example, when moving to the right with a similar angle of displacement the horse in half-pass at the canter crosses the legs much less than at the walk or trot. While right shoulder-in complicates but straightens the right-lead canter, half-pass to the right encourages it, possibly to the point of making the horse crooked.

Canter and half-pass belong together and favour one another. Gustav Steinbrecht is right again when calling the half-pass the 'canter position'.

To sum up, one can say that the shoulder-in solves problems, while the half-pass poses them. One is as natural as the other sophisticated. The first is more a training exercise, the latter a test. Thus, one is justified in considering the shoulder-in a basic exercise to which one returns over and over again in the course of education and in elevating the half-pass, proof of a conquered difficulty, to the rank of an 'air'. Lateral work that is well thought through consists always of performing numerous transitions between the two positions – so that the shoulder-in becomes to the half-pass like the life-belt to swimming.

III Perfection

Once the horse has relaxed his top line through the use of the neck extension and work on circles, then improved his lateral flexibility and resolved any issues of straightness through work on two tracks, he is now ready to begin the exercises which shift weight to the hindquarters; thereby enabling collection and with it the possibility of stylising the gaits.

Travers on the circle
Definition
The position is the same as in the half-pass but now performed on the circle and one takes care to remain on three tracks to maintain forward

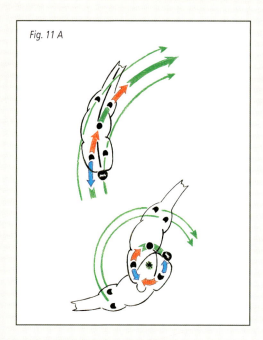

Fig. 11 A

Travers on the circle leads to the pirouette

movement. With this exercise one begins to explore the spectrum of possibilities of rotation around the hindquarters.

Advantages
If the horse is already accustomed to travers on a straight line, he should be able to make the transition to travers on a large circle without any real difficulty.

Because the forehand moves on a bigger circle than the hindquarters, the forelegs must cover more ground than the hind legs. To achieve this, the horse must lighten the forehand and load his quarters. The exercise therefore encourages the horse to engage both hind legs under his body and flex his lumbar spine as well as elevating and rounding from the base of his neck. In other words, to begin to collect himself.

With progressive practice the circle can be reduced to the pirouette: the pure rotation of the forehand around the hindquarters where the inside hind leg becomes the point of rotation as it steps in place. This places very high demands on the horse's ability to collect. The exercise is performed at first at a collected walk, at the trot it tends to produce the piaffe, while at the canter it encourages the canter in place.

Rein-back
Definition
Performed correctly, the rein-back is a diagonal walking pace whereby the functioning of the whole movement apparatus is reversed. Whereas the body is normally pushed in a forwards direction by the rearward disengagement of the hind legs, it is drawn to the rear by the motion of the hind legs engaging forwards under the body.

Advantages
Rein-back places significant loading on the muscles of the abdominal ring (abdominal and psoas muscles). This causes increased flexion of the lumbar spine, a lowering of the haunches and a shortening of the diagonal bases of support from the

Rein-back

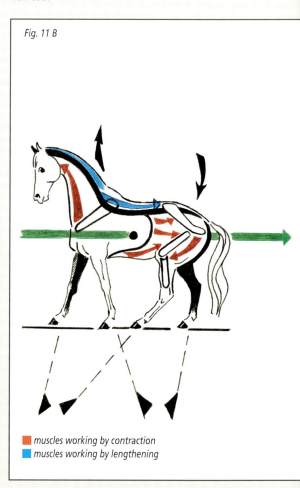

Fig. 11 B

■ *muscles working by contraction*
■ *muscles working by lengthening*

Piaffe

Pesade

rear. This stretching of the longissimus muscles from the rear and the transfer of weight onto the hindquarters promote the elevation of the base of the neck and an unloading of the forehand. Approaching the vertical, the brachio-cephalic muscles contribute to the elevation of the steps.

Properly performed, with frequent transitions to lively paces, reining-back forms a key practice on the way to collection. It rounds the horse, places him on the hindquarters and brings elevation to the steps and expression to the gaits.

Piaffe

With progressive development in collection the horse begins to 'prend du tride', an old French expression that has fallen into disuse but that still has no equivalent and which signifies that the gaits are becoming cadenced and expressive due to 'flexible and active' haunches. Thus the rider can obtain the 'school walk', the 'school canter' and 'school trot', the stylisation of which culminates in the passage.

Nevertheless, the exercise which serves best to promote this 'tride' is without doubt the piaffe, which… 'puts the horse in a nice position and gives him a noble and elevated step; and which makes the movements of his shoulders free and powerful and the springs of the haunches soft and supple: all these qualities one seeks in a parade horse and for the training of a nice passage' (François Robichon de La Guérinière).

When the horse shows enough flexibility and straightness associated with a constant desire to go forward, notable by the quality of rein-back to trot transitions, the gait can gain in elevation what it loses in length of stride to the point of 'passage in place' and becomes the piaffe. The full power of the haunches pushes upwards. All the joints flex elastically. The horse springs from one diagonal to the other with round, 'measured' and majestically cadenced steps. The nobility of this 'air' should not lead us to forget its value as an exercise. A good piaffe can arise only from superior balance and impulsion. It is the 'proof' of collection and the equestrian 'state of grace' from which everything proves to be possible, because it produces the unstable balance with full impulsion.

The pesade

Complete mastery of balance and the ultimate degree of collection are reached in the pesade.

If the rider is able to increase the engagement of the hind legs beyond that which is strictly necessary for the piaffe, there comes a point where the forehand lightens so much that the horse can lift his forelegs off the ground and balance for a few moments on his hindquarters. Like every classical air deserving of the name, the pesade is also a valuable training exercise …

'One makes use of this exercise to teach the horse to lightly lift his forehand with gracefully bent forelegs and to become firmer on the hindquarters.'
(La Guérinière)

Anyone who can really produce the piaffe can proceed to the pesade and anyone who achieves it strengthens the piaffe. Thus, this air is not an exclusive specialisation but rather a continuation.

Summary

With every horse at liberty and with every horse that has not yet undergone any education under saddle, its motion is determined by the base of the neck and the shoulders. At the beginning of training, the control of the horse in forward motion depends on appropriate positioning of the neck which loses its natural 'S' curve and becomes stabilised at the base.

In the end, the fully trained horse is characterised by motion that has its home in the hindquarters.

Characteristics of the basic gaits in training

The walk

The walk is a symmetrical, regular, four-beat gait without any suspension phase.

At the walk, the horse's balance is extremely stable since every single stride comprises four phases of support on three legs separated by four phases of support on two legs (two diagonal and two lateral). The neck plays an active role as a balancing arm.

This quiet, slow and stable gait allows the rider to act with precision upon a receptive horse. It is the gait in which one can most easily de-contract and resolve resistances. The rider has only moderate influence on the balance of the horse, however, whose body weight, always solidly supported on two or three legs, is not very mobilised in this gait. Furthermore, the natural free play of the neck, so indispensable for an active walk results, of course, in a lack of fixity of the forehand which limits the degree by which the horse can be mise en main

Fig. 12

Development of the 'Equus Velocipedus' from starting, via neck extension to pesade

(see 'The rein aids', page 66). By basing the horse's education upon this gait, therefore, one risks sacrificing impulsion for precision.

The trot

The trot is a symmetrical, diagonalised gait with two suspension phases. The horse springs from one diagonal leg pair to the other and is, therefore, in a relatively unstable yet constant and dynamic balance which the rider can readily influence. Furthermore, the trot is the only gait in which the head is naturally relatively fixed. This quality designates it the basic gait for the schooling of the mise en main in a way that respects forward movement and, in fact, arises from it.

In addition, three simple observations confirm the essential role of the trot in rebalancing the horse:
• Study of the horse's locomotion shows that all transitions between gaits depend upon a diagonal base of support.
• While reining-back, the 'reverse gear' (without suspension phase) which assumes a reflux of weight towards the hindquarters, the horse naturally chooses diagonal steps.
• If the horse moves under the influence of any kind of excitement while remaining in place, he spontaneously takes up diagonal steps – and begins to piaffe …

So, nature clearly shows that the horse is best disposed to manage his balance when taking diagonal strides. Hence, the trot inarguably constitutes a key gait for developing the horse's balance.

Canter

The canter is a rocking, asymmetrical three-beat, gait with a jump phase. It is characterised by the fact that one lateral pair of legs is carried ahead of the opposite lateral pair about two-thirds of the time during each stride.

In the canter the neck plays a critical role as a balancing arm. It stretches and lowers as the horse bascules his haunches toward the forehand and rises again as the shoulders rock back towards the hindquarters. While the canter is not, a priori, a favourable gait for the development of the mise en main it does, on the other hand, offer the advantage of working the horse's whole top line in the vertical plane by alternating flexions and extensions.

As a training gait, however, the canter does throw up some problems:
• Base of support and balance constantly changing – therefore difficult to master.
• Speed tends to excite and quickly leads to tiredness.
• The asymmetrical movements of the limbs accentuate any asymmetries and any lack of lateral suppleness or straightness.

For all of these reasons one must probably regard the canter as a means by which to test the progress achieved at the walk and the trot rather than as a basic training gait.

To summarise the general use of the gaits in the education of the riding horse in a pithy formula, one could say that it is convenient to:
• introduce at the walk;
• school and perfect at the trot;
• test and confirm at the canter.

Pioneers of tradition

Just as L'Hotte had to fight for thirty years and attain the rank of General to be able to add the rising trot to the cavalry regulations, Danloux needed twenty years and the rank of a colonel to gain acceptance of the forward jumping seat developed by Caprilli. This certainly explains his famous words: 'the worship of tradition does not exclude the love of progress.' Although their respective experiences show that they had to fight even more against conservative sluggishness than against the worship of tradition! In any case, both are among the pioneers of horsemanship to whom we shall be forever indebted.

For good measure, one must admit that Danloux's quote turns out to be perfectly reversible. Since even if 'the worship of tradition does not exclude the love of progress', the worship of progress, on the other hand, can exclude the love of tradition. Thus the founding of the Cadre Noir in the nineteenth century, in response to the military necessities of the time and a 'galloping Anglo-mania', gave sport riding a salutary and decisive impulse. Wonderful – but at the same time it became popular, under the influence of snobbery and intellectual laziness, to abolish as outdated everything that had gone before. The 'modernists', as keen on innovation as they were quick to disparage, consigned the 'ancients' to a kind of equestrian Stone Age. As someone noted: 'No more fathers, only sons!'

This unfortunate breaking of a valuable 'Ariadne's thread' had multiple consequences, some of which can be regarded as symptomatic. By 1970 the French dressage championships were contested without the piaffe or passage. At the beginning of the 1970s the International Equestrian Federation (FEI) considered very seriously removing both these airs from Olympic tests. The pesade, the highest expression of collection and the basis of the classical airs above ground, has disappeared from the French riding scene. All in all, and despite the Baucherist intermezzo, educated riding has changed in a few decades from a culture of collection to a culture of extensions and flying changes across the diagonal. If we applied the language of the sociologists to this development of riding, we would say there was 'cultural regression'.

As the famous researcher, Konrad Lorenz, said:

'A culture rests on a balance between two mechanisms: acquisition of new information and conservation of knowledge. They are both necessary. Tradition represents the mechanism of knowledge conservation.'

Since we are talking about cultivation, perhaps I may be permitted an agricultural metaphor! Clearing new ground is a good thing, but will only lead to a real expansion of one's territory if the proven old fields are not left fallow at the same time.

> 'Equestrian tradition should be, as with all others, living and pure. Is that the case? Who could say so?'
> *(Jean Saint-Fort-Paillard, L'Équitation)*

Of course, when Alain Francqueville suggested that I work with Odin on the creation of a historical presentation for the gala shows of the Cadre Noir, he already had a project in mind. He knew it would require irrefutable arguments combined with an undeniable sense of diplomacy to introduce an Iberian stallion into the presentations which had been absolutely dominated by Thoroughbreds, Anglo Arabs and Selles Français for ever. The brilliant idea consisted of breaking up the presentations of the Cadre Noir with a review of the origins of the equestrian connection with the town of Saumur.

A little history: after the announcement of the Edict of Nantes by Henry IV, Saumur became one of the 'sanctuaries' of the reformed church. Duplessis-Mornay founded a Protestant Academy there which flourished, educating young nobles in what were considered the distinguished arts of that time: philosophy, mathematics, dance, fencing, horse riding, etc. A Monsieur de Saint-Vual taught, to the letter, according to the precepts emanating from the Italian Renaissance and brilliantly transmitted by Salomon de La Broue and Antoine de Pluvinel (riding master of the Duc d'Anjou, future Henry III, then of the Dauphin and future Louis XIII). Now, the Spanish jennets were, without doubt, the most prized horses in all academies … Thanks indeed to the enlightened tolerance of good King Henry!

So much for the historical justification. Moreover, I was not yet a member of the Cadre Noir, and because the representation of the Protestant Academy was included in the plan at the beginning, one could view it simply as an experimental interlude or if one prefers, a kind of cultural aperitif!

The production of this review required a huge investment in research and planning. Based on the engravings and sketches from Antoine de Pluvinel's 'L'Instruction du Roy en l'exercice de monter à cheval', we had to develop a script that faithfully reflected the aims and methods of equitation of the late sixteenth and early seventeenth centuries. At that time the riding master had to train a parade and battle horse: brilliant in polite company, and as dependable in war as in the carrousels.

With the help of two pages it began with lateral work in all three basic gaits around a single pillar … then moved on to voltes (squares on two tracks with a quarter pirouette in every corner), then continuing with passades: charges back and forth at the gallop on the same straight line, turning with a half pirouette at each end. It all culminated in a series of attacks with a sword or lance in hand, recreating the combat horse's training exercises. The presentation ended with piaffe sequences between the pillars then riding out in passage. With a final pesade we would have completed our mission perfectly, but Odin was not yet capable of that. I had already trained two other horses to this air but I did not know whether he had enough strength to one day reach such a degree of collection.

While preparing the necessary equipment posed no major difficulties, one could not say the same for our principal character. Charging straight towards a post from which rings or 'heads' hung ready to be speared with lance or sword, with reins in one hand and without any guiding fence, then turning about in a half pirouette and repeating the whole 'circus' five or six times, was no easy business. Add to this an easily excitable horse in changing light conditions, 'persecuted' by the beam of a floodlight – and everything aggravated still further by his heartfelt calls to his stable mates in his anxiety over being separated from them – and one has quite a tricky situation!

We practised a lot, often rehearsing at night in the floodlights … and on 5 October 1986, on the occasion of the annual gala evening of the Friends of the Cadre Noir, took the plunge.

For the performance we hired some theatrical costumes from Paris, and Alain Francqueville concocted a commentary of remarkable depth and precision.

There we were, Odin and I, completely dressed up 'à la Louis XIII'. 'The absolute epitome of Pluvinel!' – or at least that was my playful answer to the banter from all around. Indeed, one could have been forgiven for thinking I was going to a fancy dress ball, but had come to the wrong address!

Nevertheless, I have known since that day what it means to have stage fright. If I had been waiting backstage at the Comédie Française for my appearance as Cyrano de Bergerac (the same costume, only without the horse and with the nose), I would have suffered no more! For me, the stakes were as great as the inexperience of my horse and I began to wonder why on earth I was doing this to myself! But there was no longer any escape, and the only remedy to my fears lay beyond the great door of the Manège des Écuyers (the main indoor performance arena at the National School of Equitation) and under the gaze of 2000 pairs of inquisitive eyes …

While awaiting my uncertain deliverance, I remembered a remark attributed to Sarah Bernhardt. One day, as a young actress boasted before her of knowing no stage fright, she answered: 'Don't worry – it will come… together with talent.' From this one can conclude first of all that talent requires 'more perspiration than inspiration', secondly that only the vain know no stage fright, and, finally, that this miserable stage fright is only a fear of disappointing, a tribute to the audacity of appearing in public and at the same time an appeal to one's modesty.

For me, the presentation went like a kind of daydream led by Alain Francqueville's confident and familiar voice. The clearest memory I can recall was a divine surprise: Odin, who could be knocked off his stride by the slightest little thing, showed practically no concern about the applause. His Highness was just born for ovations!

In the course of the conversations after the show, Alain Francqueville and I received much encouragement; especially from the words of Colonel de Saint-André, Écuyer en chef of the Cadre Noir until 1972, a personality who made a strong impression on the School and whose opinion was still much respected. I subsequently had several enriching and spirited conversations with him during which I learned, among other things, that he

Pioneers of tradition

Riding exercises during the 'Protestant Academy' presentation

Charging in the opposite direction after a half pirouette at the canter

was seconded for some years as an instructor to the cavalry school in Mafra, and came back fluent in Portuguese!

It was decided that we should appear again during a special gala evening marking the occasion of the Saumur international three-day event in April 1986 – after making use of the winter break to perfect the presentation.

From then on, events jostled for space in the calendar. The historical review, now officially christened the 'Protestant Academy', would figure in the programme of two important trips of the Cadre Noir planned in May and June 1986. Life certainly seems to like a touch of irony, because while the second presentation took place in the castle of Saint-Germain-en-Laye (where Napoleon had set up a cavalry school between 1809 and 1814), the first would take us to the heart of the great stables of the Château de Versailles! On his first trip from Saumur, Odin would accompany the Cadre Noir to this hallowed site, considered the cradle of French classical horsemanship. Was that a knowing wink from the spirits of the Écuyers of the Age of Enlightenment, whom I held in such high esteem?

For this event Alain Francqueville persuaded the School to finance the acquisition of some splendid costumes which were produced by a big name in stage and film production, Daniel Ogier. There was no doubt, our experiment had a future.

I have three major recollections of the trip to Versailles.

The first contains nothing pleasant. Odin proved to be hellishly bad to transport. In spite of all conceivable precautions, he would not stand still, rocked dripping with sweat from one leg to the other and was in danger of killing himself with the force of his unbridled gesticulations. Nothing helped.

On our return from Versailles, he had lost at least thirty kilos. As a result it was decided to give him a tranquiliser before every journey to prevent the worst. This remained necessary for two or three years.

The second recollection is happier. The first two presentations took place in the evening, the last on Sunday afternoon. Seating tribunes were built up around a sand arena in the shape of a horseshoe and the background was formed by nothing less than the marvelous facade of the main stable built by Mansart. Passing through the arcades of these historically significant buildings then arriving in the arena to the rhythms of a march by Lully and seeing beyond the stands the illuminated facade of the Château de Versailles with the equestrian statue of Louis XIV was unforgettable, an unusually moving moment.

The third recollection of this event is this remarkable photograph, taken during the course of the Sunday afternoon presentation. It was the work of Alain Laurioux, to whose talent I owe all the photos which decorate this book. The piaffe in front of the gates of the 'Grande Écurie du Roy' would later become one of the pictures selected to form posters for sale to visitors at the National School of Equitation.

The trip to Saint-Germain-en-Laye in June was a further confirmation, and the season ended with a gala performance for the Friends of the Cadre Noir, on 18 October. I began the evening as usual in my costume 'à la Louis XIII'. I finished the evening in the black uniform of the Cadre Noir, however, to present in long reins a Selle Français mare whose name already spoke volumes: Prétentieuse.

In fact, on this day I was officially presented with my black and gold cravache (schooling whip), the symbol of my admission to the Cadre Noir. Several friends and relatives came to share this honourable moment with me and to congratulate me. One should never forget those who sincerely rejoice in your success, because they give you reason to continue ... and a certain obligation.

Piaffe in front of the doors of the Grande Écurie du Roy in Versailles

Work on the lunge

Whether one uses lungeing to prepare a horse for riding, to exercise a horse that cannot be ridden, or simply as a warm-up before working under saddle, the same rules always apply.

There is a primitive conception of lungeing which has to be rejected from the start: the idea that it consists of condemning a horse to run in circles until he is tired, so that one can more quickly assert oneself on the back of the exhausted animal. Apart from the inelegance of such a procedure, one can easily imagine the physical and psychological damage that it would produce – and which can sometimes be irreversible. 'To proceed quickly one must take one's time.'

Good lungeing wins the horse's trust, gives him the opportunity to let off some steam, it disciplines and prepares the horse to carry the weight of the rider and be guided on both reins in the three basic gaits.

Aids

The voice

The voice is the most important aid available to the trainer in all work from the ground. The cavesson, lunge line, long reins and whip are only a supplement or means of correction. Hence, quite special care must be applied when educating the horse to the voice. The horse possesses remarkably sharp hearing and an excellent memory. By associative reflexes he will quickly come to 'understand' what the trainer requires of him. The voice is also the least aggressive means of intervention.

Use of the voice

Use clear, sober language that is well differentiated in two ways: terms and intonation. Conditioning the horse requires that the trainer uses the same expressions for the same requests, and repeats them frequently. Long, drawn-out syllables with deep, subdued tones have a reassuring effect: restraining aids. Short, sharp syllables in higher tones, on the other hand, are more stimulating: driving aids.

Examples:
- 'Walk-on', in a sharp tone to begin walking.
- 'Trot', in a dry tone to take the trot.
- 'Gal-lop' or 'can-ter', in either case separating the two syllables.
- To avoid confusion, tongue clicking should only be used to keep the horse up to the gait at which he is already going.
- 'Oooh ... tro-o-o-t', in a long, drawn-out and low tone, to bring the horse back from the canter.
- 'Oooh ... wa-a-a-lk', uttered in the same way, to bring him back from the trot, later even to return to the walk from the canter.

• 'Oooh ... halt!', in a firm tone to produce an immediate halt, firstly from the walk, then the trot and eventually the canter.
• A very long and softly drawn out 'Oooooh ... oooooh ...', can be used to calm and slow the horse within a given gait.

Through precision and rigour, the trainer will soon enable his horse to understand him.

The lunge whip

Just as for spurs when working under saddle, the lunge whip or schooling whip should only be regarded as supporting aids during work from the ground. They are additional aids which provide a means to punish laziness or to win back the horse's attention, but above all to refine the obedience to the voice or leg.

Using the lunge whip

If the young horse is to respect the whip, it is important that he does not fear it. One should not undertake anything, above all with a sensitive, fearing animal, before he accepts the touch of the whip all over his body while remaining calm and immobile.

The obedience to the voice is the result of the following precautions with the use of the whip:
• Never use the whip before or without giving an order with the voice. Calling a pupil to order when he has no idea at all what one expects from him is a mistake on the part of the teacher.
• Accompany the voice with a moderate, but immediate effect of the whip every time the original request does not produce a clear and immediate reaction.
• Cease the action of the whip and voice as soon as a satisfactory response is obtained.
• Correct any unsolicited slowing down with the whip. If the trainer incessantly aids a lazy or negligent horse with the voice he will begin to ignore it.
• Graduation of interventions with the whip: one must take care to accompany the horse with the whip held very quietly and pointing at the hocks. Depending on the circumstances and the horse's temperament, the trainer may make measured interventions while limiting them always to only what is strictly necessary.
• Raising the whip in the direction of hindquarters represents an urgent request for a response.
• Swishing the whip, so that the end of the string touches the thigh of the hind leg, represents a serious admonition.
• Flicking the whip so that the string wraps from the back to the front around the hindquarters represents a severe punishment of disobedience.

In all cases, the trainer should use the whip only with the aim of being able to do without it as soon as possible.

Cavesson and lunge line

Under the pretext that a thick cavesson is as ineffective with lazy horses that one wants to have pay attention as it is with hot horses which one would like to have respect for it, countless riders fasten the lunge line directly to the bit. However more or less complex the device may look (the lunge line passing over the poll or saddle, with a bitting rig or directly attached to the bit rings etc.) – there is nothing good to say about this practice.

In fact, these methods are incompatible with even the most elementary consideration for the horse's mouth. One knows how difficult it is just to maintain a steady, light connection with the horse if the rider, united with his mount, has only one metre of rein between himself and the mouth ... what should one expect if the person is ten metres away from the horse? The force necessary just to take contact with eight or ten metres of lunge line alone represents an attack on the mouth.

If we add that, by definition, the horse runs at semi-liberty on the lunge and he may decide to let off some steam ... some messing about, bucking or racing off is common, at least at the beginning of the work ... and that, in the end, 70 to 80 kilos of homo-sapiens swings on ten metres of line from the mouth of 500 to 600 kilos of horse! Pain triggers the flight instinct, which again increases the pressure on the mouth, etc. This is simply a vicious circle! Finally, let's consider incidents that can always happen: the horse gets a foreleg over a sagging lunge line, or it steps on it, or the horse breaks loose and the line gets caught, etc. All of these can result in cut-through tongues or a broken jaw. Worst-case scenarios usually never happen, yet are always a possibility; nothing obliges us to tempt fate!

The reasonable solution, that is to say, one that is efficient and respects the mouth, is to use a real cavesson – as did the old masters who,

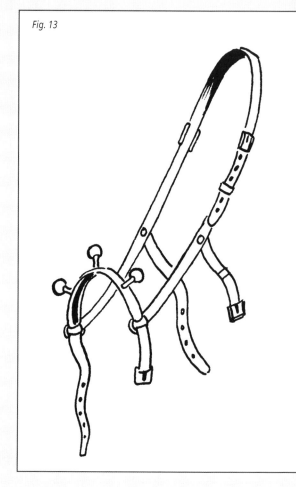

Fig. 13

Lunge cavesson

it is true, didn't canter on three legs or teach tempi-changes or jump over mountains, but nevertheless did have some experience.

In the seventeenth and eighteenth centuries the cavesson was used in all the academies of Europe, but since then has become consigned to the history books. Nowadays christened the 'Spanish cavesson', since it is still traditionally used in that country, it is also to be recommended to the north of the Pyrenees.

It consists of a U-shaped metal piece adapted to the shape of the nosebone, and padded more or less thickly according to the degree of severity desired. When fitted correctly, with a jowl strap to prevent rotation, it sits quite high so as not to have an effect on the end or the cartilage of the nose bone. It enables the trainer to bring any horse under control in a few lessons and to discipline even a combative stallion. This is infinitely better than painful jerks on the bit that result only in spoiling the mouth, destroying trust and provoking the horse's defences.

Graduation of the effects of the cavesson

The lunge line (preferably rope or strong cotton tape, rather than the lighter materials which lack sufficient deadweight for the exact transmission of the aids) must stay in touch with the horse and accompany his movements.

If the horse does not react to a request to slow down the pace:
• Firstly, vibrate the lunge line to attract the horse's attention.
• If still no response, a vigorous raising of the hand indicates a final warning.
• In the end, if necessary, make one or more lively downwards jerks of the lunge line. This is the most severe call to order and punishment of negligence.

Mobility of the trainer

If the trainer wants his horse to remain attentive, he should not stand statically in the middle, but should move on a small circle. Thus he can remain at or behind the level of the haunches and have the horse 'in front of himself': a position that helps drive the horse forwards.

The position of the trainer who always moves along with the horse becomes, in the end, the principal aid, because the horse at the end of the lunge line modifies his movements according to those of his partner. Little by little the cavesson and whip become merely aids or means of correction, and the horse moves 'at liberty on parole'.

Auxiliary reins

Work on the lunge is really only effective if it straightens the horse on the circle, if it stretches the top line and causes the horse to take contact with the bit by extending his neck. The help of auxiliary reins is necessary, therefore, with some precautions:
• Soft bit with a thick mouthpiece.
• Very progressive adjustment: the auxiliary reins must not be used to force the horse into the required posture but rather to create at most an opposition if the horse deviates from it too much. Thus one can achieve a light contact in correct posture, without compulsion.
• Because the neck extension is achieved through lateral stretching, only auxiliary reins which permit completely free mobility in the lateral plane are acceptable. Fixed side reins, therefore, are prohibited.
• At the walk and the canter the horse must be able to use the full range of movement of his neck – otherwise he will jab his mouth against the bit with every stride. Should this happen, one risks disturbing the purity and regularity of the gaits (ambling walk, four-beat or running canter). So here again, fixed side reins are unsuitable. They could be useful, perhaps, at the trot and when schooling for collection during work in-hand – but that is another story.
• In order that the horse works 'on the bit' and not 'against the bit', the horse must tighten the auxiliary reins horizontally – in the direction of movement, in other words.

Fig. 14

Yes – 'on' the bit

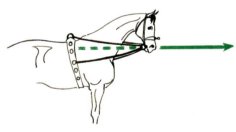

Yes – 'on' the bit

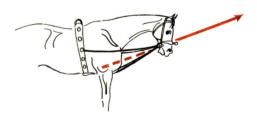

No – 'against' the bit

Correct attachment of auxiliary reins

Fig. 15

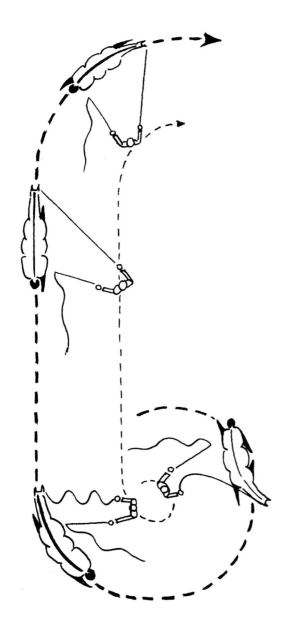
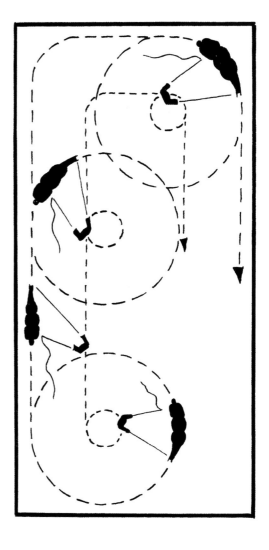
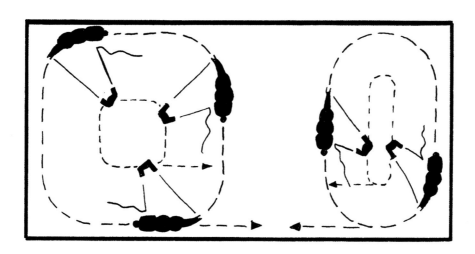

Lungeing on various figures

In summary, for auxiliary reins to be compatible with neck extension in lively gaits, they must be of 'variable geometry'.

The easiest solution is to attach a universal running rein to the upper ring of a lunge roller so that it can slide freely and adjust the length and the height of the lower lateral attachment according to the posture desired. Thus the horse can be framed and encouraged to stretch to the bit while at the same time his neck is allowed a relatively high degree of freedom; preserving his desire to go forward and avoiding provoking any defence against excessive constriction.

Gymnastic development

While lungeing, the aim is to promote forwards movement and stretching of the top line. The extension of the neck is achieved above all through repeated lateral flexions and the auxiliary reins merely give a frame.

Statement

By nature, the horse turns by losing his balance: he allows the lunge line to sag, falls in to the centre of the circle, inverts his neck and bends it outwards, while simultaneously carrying his haunches to the outside. With a horse that is naturally bent to the left, this behaviour appears more markedly on the right rein.

If one tries to bend him by pulling his head inwards, the horse tightens the circle, falls inwards even more without bending, and the hindquarters fall out even more markedly: the remedy is worse than the evil!

The judicious solution comprises of firstly sending the horse's shoulders out so that they are aligned with the hindquarters once again, while at the same time the horse re-establishes a proper contact with the lunge line. Only after that can one use the lunge line to achieve a suitable bend of the neck.

Means

By having his horse leave the circle and sending him forwards on a curve of greater diameter the trainer can cause him to re-establish the correct contact at the end of the lunge line. The trainer encourages his horse to do so by frequently leaving the circle at a tangent himself and moving in a straight line while sending the horse away by undulations of the lunge line. If necessary, he points his lunge whip at the horse's shoulder, even going so far as to clearly touch it with the lash if required.

To summarise, the horse will be working correctly on the lunge when it preserves the light contact on the line at all times and follows the circle, ready at any time to increase the diameter or to move off at a tangent.

One can see, then, that any well thought through gymnastic programme, not to mention any work that is lively and varied, must consist of a constantly changing mixture of circles and straight lines. Hence the sacrosanct 'lunge circle' is the least suitable way of achieving these ends and engenders only fatigue, pointless routine and a dull horse. The indoor or outdoor arena is much more suitable because it allows all variations: voltes and straight lines on the track, direction changes across the centreline, etc, all enriched with frequent transitions between and within the gaits; all opportunities to refine the horse's obedience to the voice.

Variations

Also on the lunge, the horse will again behave differently on each rein according to his natural asymmetry – let's consider once again the example of a horse that is naturally bent to the left:

- On the right rein, the horse falls inwards and the lunge line goes slack. Work on very large circles in a very lively tempo (taking advantage of the effects of centrifugal force). Once achieved, ask for a clear bend.
- On the left rein the horse finds it easy to bend his neck but may exaggerate it, which leads to falling out through the outside shoulder (the disadvantage of the effect of centrifugal force). One must reduce this phenomenon by moderating the tempo and using the effects of the walls to straighten the horse with limited bend.

The application of these methods in a carefully considered manner allows the horse to gradually work more and more symmetrically – the first contribution to straightening.

Introduction to long reins

Often one hears or reads that long reins belong to driving, and do substantially more harm than good with the riding horse (causing him to become hard-mouthed, to overflex, to go on the forehand, etc). In reality, it is not long reins by themselves that cause these problems, but using them badly. As with all other effective aids (curb, spurs, whip) one could also describe them as 'a razor blade in the hand of a monkey'.

Used with care after some intelligent work on the lunge, however, they can be of value. The following additional steps are necessary.

A Introduction with the cavesson

Just as with lungeing, the protection of the horse's mouth must also be given prime consideration before any other. Hence, the German expression 'Doppellonge' (double-lungeing) is spot on!

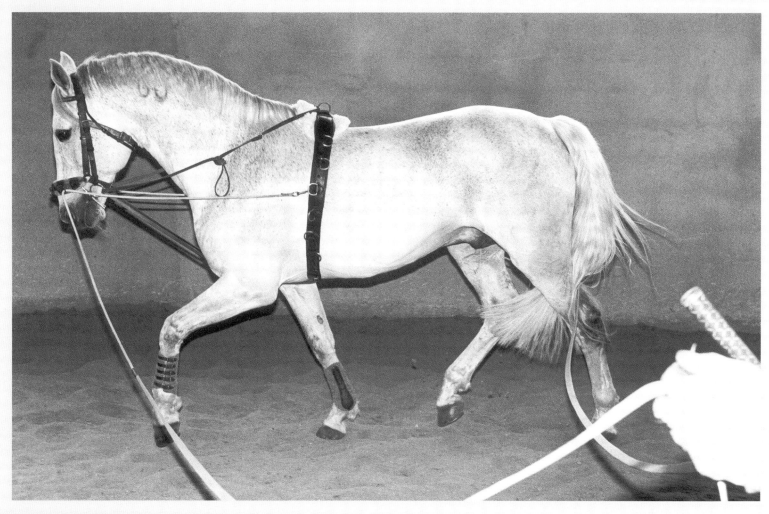

Long reins attached to a cavesson

1. Attach the long reins to a padded cavesson, auxiliary reins to the bit

Reversing the attachment of the inside rein, by passing it through the cavesson before attaching it to the roller, provides a clear but painless sideways-bending effect. The outside rein runs over the back. The lines are attached to the roller in such a way that they lie horizontal if the horse goes in the correct posture.

2. Accustom the horse to the feel of the outside rein around the haunches

Should the horse kick out or want to run, there are no negative consequences for the mouth, and trust will develop by itself.

3. Symmetrical attachment of the long reins and first direction changes

At this point, all the dressage figures become possible. The trainer can vary the bend at will, ask for counter-bending, control or displace the haunches. The overall posture is preserved by the auxiliary reins.

B Transition to working on the bit

Once the horse has become accustomed to working in the cavesson, repeat all of the exercises described above. Use a snaffle bit that cannot be pulled through the mouth: for example, one with Fulmer cheeks.

1. Reversed attachment of the inside rein

Opening-rein effect which bends the neck laterally – instead of an effect of opposition which risks causing overflexion. Outside rein passes over the back and not round the croup, because otherwise the pendulum movement of the outside hind leg would be transmitted to the mouth, particularly at the canter. If it is necessary to keep the hindquarters from escaping, one can attach the outside line to the cavesson once again.

2. Reins attached symmetrically and changes of rein

Only to be attempted once the horse is equally flexible on both reins in order that the opposing

Work on the lunge

effect of the inside rein will no longer provoke any resistance and can achieve a lateral bending of the neck without leading to overflexion in the longitudinal plane.

3. Working without auxiliary reins
When the horse stays at the end of the reins, on the bit, bends without resistances and follows all the trainer's movements – there is nothing stopping the trainer from removing the auxiliary reins and working close behind the horse.

In conclusion

In a systematic and regular programme (once a week, for example) the horse can be introduced to the long reins little by little, some variation being introduced to the work and the horse gradually prepared to accept them in more delicate situations. This was the case with Odin.

By contrast, if long reins are used abruptly and without preparation to try to solve problems in the course of training, then one is relying on their power more than their advantages, resorting to force, and this will surely lead to more difficulties than success.

Long reins attached to the bit

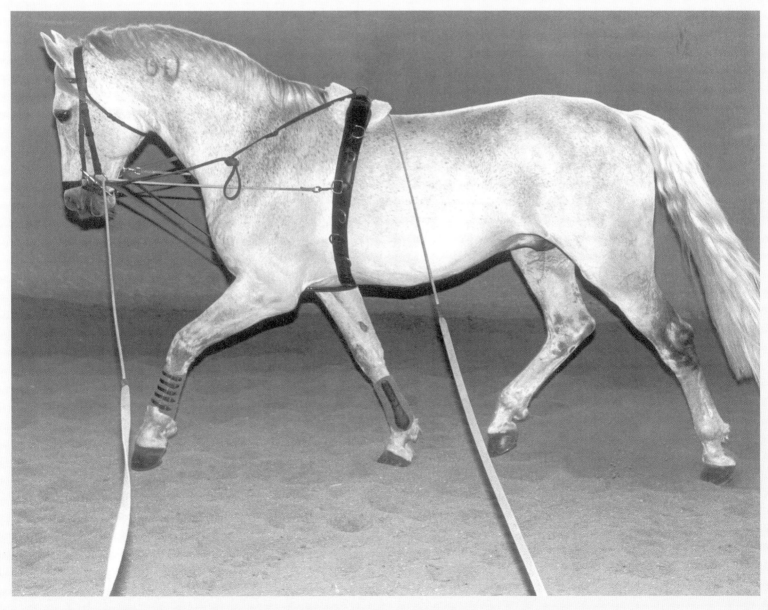

The jester

The French word saltimbanque (jester) has more than one meaning: in the literal sense, someone who performs acrobatic or circus tricks in public; in the figurative sense, a fool or charlatan!

Asked over and over again to appear in unusual and impractical places and under unpredictable, risky conditions, Odin was certainly a jester in the literal sense, often before an audience ranging from a couple of hundred to several thousand people. The main challenge was to avoid Odin becoming a jester in the other sense – since all of the pejorative associations would have fallen back on me personally. But, after all, 'a victory without danger is a triumph without glory'.

The theatre

Odin owes his debut treading the boards to my wife; a ballet and tap dancing instructor who frequently dreams up and organises performances for her pupils. In June 1987, the chosen subject was 'the public park'. With the help of some impromptu scenery on the stage of the magnificent old theatre of Saumur, she wanted to show the life and people in a public park: the park keeper, people in deckchairs, sportsmen, children playing, lovers etc.

Since her imagination and her audacity know no bounds, she fantasised about a little girl falling asleep on a bench and dreaming of a Western in which – just for once – cowboys and Indians danced together in peaceful harmony! Very pertinently, she thought to herself: 'No self-respecting Western without horses ...', only to decide, not without some impertinence, that Odin and I would be quite capable of taking on the role! Since my desire to make her happy and accept the affectionate challenge outweighed my doubts and awareness of the risk which I would be taking on, I agreed to this mad prank.

In two performances I would have to convince Odin to pass through the colonnades of the theatre under the stage, to enter it via a very steep passageway barely one and a half metres wide, to cross the stage in passage and then turn in piaffe-pirouette, before making the return journey, all in the midst of a dozen dancers in full swing and to disappear again without missing a beat, because, of course, the show must go on!
'I can't promise you that is possible', I said.
'I'm sure you can do it', answered my wife.

First performance

In fact, it went without too much trouble. An anti-slip mat guarded against any dangerous sliding. To make the going even more secure, I had new nails put in Odin's shoes whose square heads worked like little crampons. I mounted and steered Odin in the intended direction and tried to let him feel my determination, but without any roughness. Step by step I forged ahead, pausing frequently in between to let him think, while I reassured and praised him, until finally we reached the stage. After a few moments of understandable worry, he played his role with a little stage fright but also the professionalism of a big actor!

I thought the job was done – but I was very much mistaken, because the most difficult part was getting him off the stage again! Not because he couldn't bear to leave the limelight ... but because he had to go down the steep, narrow, poorly illuminated passageway again! Nothing worked, and I had to guide him backwards three or four times before I could get him to go in to it forwards. Thank goodness for rein-back ...!

Second performance

After the achievements of the day before were confirmed, we had to work out to the second the time needed to appear on stage without having to wait in the narrow confines behind the scenes. The operation was awkward, but feasible.

On the evening of the performance, after a warm-up on the shores of the Loire, Odin and I set out to conquer the Wild West and the theatre of Saumur. Dressed by John Ford and shod like a tap dancer, Odin stepped up and performed a 'number' of which neither John Wayne nor Fred Astaire would have been ashamed!

My wife's show was such a success that it was repeated about six months later – and Odin was present again. This time as an old trouper of the touring theatre!

To be honest, I was glad when it was over, because I was aware that I had drawn deeply from his reserves of trust. In Alain Laurioux's snapshot, one can clearly see from the expression of his slightly bulging eye how disturbing it was for him. Another sign: Odin's mouth became worryingly mute ... no trace of légèreté! I informed my wife that Odin had given us such a gift that we could not ask it of him again. She absolutely understood.

The circus

One day in 1988 Colonel Durand, director of the School, asked me quite abruptly:
'Do you know that eight days ago an Italian circus put up its tents in Saumur?'
'Actually, I have seen posters ...'
'Do you know, they are running a circus school and preparing amateurs from the area to show their tricks in tomorrow evening's presentation?'
'Now, that I didn't know ...'
'I have been invited along and find it a pity that the School will not be represented at the performance!'
His eyes shone so craftily that I could easily guess what was coming. He didn't keep me waiting long.
'Could you not show your horse?'
'I fear I lack the time to prepare something, Colonel. It's only tomorrow evening. And what should I wear? Which music should I choose? Still ... I could always go and check the place out, have a chat with the people there and see what might be possible!'
'Good! You do that. You have carte blanche!'

Carte blanche ... the famous freedom to do anything, that so often means one ends up doing everything!

I immediately made an appointment to show Odin the circus tent the next morning. While I rode him in the 'big top', different circus tunes were

'West Side Piaffe' on the stage of the Saumur theatre

played for me. I tried to select the simplest ones with the rhythms that best fitted the different gaits. We agreed the order and duration of some pieces.

A good part of the afternoon was spent searching for someone who could lend me a top hat and a frock coat in my size, because my aim was to honour the circus riders, without giving up the characteristic dignity of the Cadre Noir.

I used the little time that remained to sketch a plan of the arena that I could use as a guide. It is not so easy to fill six or seven minutes in a manège without repetition or running out of ideas. On a thirteen-metre diameter circle one goes round pretty quickly! No matter how useful a circle is when working the horse, it is just as restricting if one is tied to it. Compared to the traditional dressage arena the circus ring is like a handkerchief. Here the horses must be presented practically without any straight lines or the possibility of extending the gaits in a state of considerable and constant collection.

Dressage riders inclined to denounce the work of circus people should try it: they will soon change their minds! One quickly realises why Franconi, Pellier, Baucher and others devised all sorts of fantasy airs to hold the interest of an audience made up predominantly of laymen. The constriction of the place in itself tempts one into inventions of dubious taste.

When it was our turn to enter the 'mini-manège', I avoided getting on my high horse and stuck as closely as possible to the programme I had previously sketched out: lateral work with original combinations at the walk, trot and canter, canter pirouettes, passage, piaffe. To round it off, pesades which Odin at that time could perform quite honourably. We left the arena in Spanish walk.

At the end of the performance, the respected grandmother of the Italian circus family told me how moved she had been to have had a representative of the Cadre Noir as a guest in her tent for the evening; and she explained to me with tears in her eyes that she had been a vaulter in her youth. Colonel Durand returned her heartfelt gratitude with his professional compliments and personal thanks.

A sketchy pesade in the circus ring

For the duration of one evening the Cadre Noir had mingled with the circus people, here in Saumur exactly where in 1843 the most famous circus rider of all, François Baucher, had shared a little of his knowledge with the instructors of the cavalry school. A modest acknowledgment, but only right and proper!

In the TV studio

In May 1992, the Cadre Noir would give an unusual guest performance in Paris: for the first time, four performances in the sports and exhibition centre at Bercy. In the course of the advertising which events of this magnitude require, the riders had to take part in a broadcast on French television's number one channel a few weeks beforehand. It was called 'Tous à la Une' ('All on one') and at that time broke the record for a prime time TV audience.

The broadcast included an interview with the new Écuyer en chef, Colonel Carde, and a presentation of two horses performing the airs above the ground in-hand. Odin, however, had the dubious honour of providing the opening pictures of the broadcast.

The director explained to me what was expected from us. After taking our place backstage, I should enter the studio, pass between the rows of a choir, then ride up a slope to a kind of small parquet area where I should present the horse on the narrow surface, surrounded by spectators and cameras. I had to insist quite strongly that the whole area would be laid out with elastic mats to prevent dangerous and ridiculous slipping! As true professionals, the studio engineers fixed the problem in the blink of an eye.

'Positions, please!'

After a brief, awkward warm-up in the car park, Odin made his entrance in passage and performed canter pirouettes, piaffe and pesades on the parquet right in front of the audience and cameras.

Piaffe live in the television studio

The initial performance having been deemed satisfactory, I was instructed to perform a second for the lighting crew ... now well! Then, after that I was told that we only needed a run-through for the sound engineers, before the dress rehearsal would take place. That would mean five repetitions in less than two hours, including the broadcast – simply not possible!

Trying carefully to avoid appearing 'cavalier', obliging enough not to be labelled a capricious country diva, I explained to the studio manager that the horse would have no strength left if we kept asking him to 'win the race in the paddock'. It was agreed that the stallion would only have to be present, without working.

Odin made the most of my circumspection, because it allowed him to get more and more used to the surroundings without getting tired. Thus, at the vital moment all his forces were available to me with a certain freshness. Everything went off very well, and I reflected that our experiences in the theatre and at the circus in Saumur must have had something to do with it!

Press conference

After the success of Bercy in 1992 our producers considered some new performances. Thus three presentations were included in the plan for November 1995.

This time, however, we would offer something new in form of an equestrian opera: the Cadre Noir would be accompanied by the French Symphony Orchestra, with the participation of the famous American singer Julia Migenes. Again, as part of the unavoidable 'promotion' of such an event in the media, a press conference was organised in the rooms of the five-star Hotel Concorde-Lafayette near the Arc de Triomphe in Paris.

Since our producers were passionate about having the active participation of a horse in this press conference, the Écuyer en chef, Colonel Carde, nominated Odin and me for this very Parisian media spectacle. So Odin spent a few hours as a guest at the Concorde-Lafayette. A 'royal box' was built for him behind the table for the press conference, next to stands from the National Riding School and the Friends of the Cadre Noir.

During this event he had to appear for a few moments in front of the blinding flashlights of the press of 'the whole of Paris'. This time we broke all records in terms of limited size, because the 'arena' consisted of a red carpet, barely five by ten metres, which was laid out on the marble floor of the hotel hall. No danger of trot extensions on the diagonal! Some lateral work at the walk, passage, piaffe, pesades: job done!

After this Lilliputian performance my friend Alain Laurioux, the photographer, complimented us with the remark: 'Odin – the only horse who can dance on a metro ticket!'

The philosophy of academic equitation

'Nothing contributes more to the knowledge of an art or science than the understanding of its own specialist terms.' *(La Guérinière)*

In other words: if we hope to collect our horse, let's begin by collecting our thoughts.

Blessed with an exceptional richness, French riding heritage is as enticing as it is irritating. Even the keenest student is up against a flood of doctrines, flowery debates and quarrels over different schools. To avoid tiresome critical interpretations as well as reductionist dogmatisms, it seems that the best opinion to consider is that of the horse ... which does not prevent one giving credit where it is due.

Academic equitation '[subjects] the horse to the progressive lessons of an aesthetic culture which is intended to develop the rhythm and harmony of his movements, whose essential characteristic features it scrupulously respects, while it strives for a stylised perfection which is transformed little by little into the airs of the High School ... In this respect, equestrian art is like choreography and the High School like the classical ballet.' *(General Decarpentry)*

To illustrate the challenge of 'dressage', it is interesting to consider the parallels between equestrian art and artistic choreography with a metaphor: the Chinese dancer. A trainer who tackles the education of a horse with the aim of reaching the High School is in the same position as a ballet teacher, who takes on a young Chinese pupil who has no notion of the ballet or the French language, but who harbours a secret hope of turning him into a dancing star.

There are two alternatives.

The first is that, using his all-powerful authority, the teacher imposes an iron discipline based on physical and mental compulsion, because he is of the opinion that his pupil will soon learn French in the course of his enforced development. This abuse of power in the service of an authoritarian image of 'discipline' denies the dignity of the pupil and breaks his personality.

Although this method sometimes achieves the desired results, they come only at the price of a lot of waste, and its products are described, except possibly by the layman, as expressionless, robotic dancers moving sadly under the control of an achievement-obsessed teacher who is more feared than respected. There is a great danger for our young Chinese that dancing, as well as the French language, will be spoiled for good!

A ballet teacher who is worthy of the name will proceed quite differently, the second alternative. After acquainting himself as much as possible with Chinese culture, in order at least to understand the temperament and behaviour of his pupil, he will make every effort to win his confidence.

First of all he will teach him the essential basic vocabulary necessary for learning to dance – systematically, word by word, by association with the appropriate movement. Calmness is, in this connection, a prerequisite for effectiveness since shouting a word that is not understood does not make it any clearer and, if it is already understood it is pointless, even idiotic to shout it loudly!

By enabling the construction of elementary sentences this vocabulary, applied alongside a thoughtful gymnastic development programme, allows the student to develop his physical capacity at the same time as his mastery of the language.

Bit by bit, communication between teacher and pupil becomes more precise and more refined until, in the end, it expresses the tiniest nuances and becomes so subtle that an observer can no longer perceive it. The results include mutual respect, commitment and affection.

Provided the talent of the latter matches the educational skill of the former, there comes a day when the teacher slips into the background to let his (Chinese!) dancing star shine.

Should ability not match ambition, our Chinese still becomes at the very least a reasonable dancer who speaks fluent French – and a well-rounded person who retains an everlasting loyalty to his teacher.

As one can see, for the trainer just as for the ballet teacher, everything depends upon the development of a language which is in turn confirmed and enriched by physical expression.

The language of the aids

Academic equitation is quite poorly described by the word 'dressage' (literally, 'training') although unfortunately that is the word in current usage. In the broadest sense 'training' describes a process of conditioning where the ends justify the means, sometimes to the point of experimentation or even cruelty. In fact it concerns the development of a coherent language between horse and rider and respect for the horse was stressed by the earliest masters.

'The horse's willing consent brings more conveniences than methods of compulsion.'
(Salomon de la Broue, 1594)

'One must be sparing with blows and generous with praise, as I will never tire of saying, to bring the horse to move and obey more from joy than from fear.'
(Antoine de Pluvinel, 1625)

To help us avoid the trap of anthropomorphism, L'Hotte also very clearly states that, 'the origin of the horse's obedience cannot lie, of course, in a desire to be nice to us, and still less in devotion to duty.' (1895). The last word on this subject goes to Alexandre Guérin (1860):

'Almost always the horse refuses to obey only because it does not understand the language of the aids.'

It is essential to define precisely the expressions of this language and to master the equestrian principles which form its syntax. Otherwise:

'By naming things badly, one increases the misery of the world.' (Albert Camus)

The degree of understanding of this language of the aids is clearly measurable thanks to the concept of légèreté, which can be simply defined by the formula in Table 3.

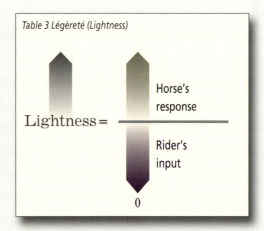

Table 3 Légèreté (Lightness)

$$\text{Lightness} = \frac{\text{Horse's response}}{\text{Rider's input}}$$

This shows that the degree of mastery of this language is proportional to the reactions of the horse and inversely proportional to the interventions of the rider. Keen obedience to aids which become smaller and smaller, tending toward zero – this is the only authentic sign of academic equitation, which some call the 'difficult ease'.

'Légèreté is limited only by the rider's tact.'
(Jean de Salins)

To build up the structure of mutually consistent conventions on which a language depends, every teacher must base his lessons on rigorous logic. This, in turn, is based on the observance of some indispensable, methodically applied principles.

Principles

• Proceed from the known to the unknown, and from the simple to the complex.
• Associate error with correction and success with praise.
• Commit to memory and improve through repetition.

Method

To make oneself understood, in the following order:
• Demand the attention of the student (take up the reins, put the legs in contact; preparatory aids, because 'a horse that is alerted is twice as ready').
• With the greatest possible precision and efficiency, formulate the problem that can most easily be solved and do not put any obstacles in the way of the response.

'Hand without legs, legs without hand'
(François Baucher).

- Refrain from chattering so as not to dull the student. This improves the chances of being heard when one asks for something (rider with an independent seat, smoothly following all the horse's movements, without any unintentional or annoying gestures, without constant use of the aids).

'Speak clearly and let him do'
(René Bacharach)

- In case of failure do not hesitate to repeat the question, without raising the voice, however … then immediately threaten a reprimand.
- In the end, if necessary, insist with complete calmness using an adequate, moderate correction. Never accept, however, that a reasonable request is allowed to go without a response, even if it is imperfect.
- Use the aids in quick 'crescendo'.
- Be quiet and listen for the answer: cease the action of the aids by lowering the hands and releasing the legs (in French: descente de mains and descente de jambes). Immediately release the aids in a 'decrescendo' to put the horse 'at liberty on parole' at the slightest hint of a response.
- Praise immediately.

'The slightest expression of obedience must be rewarded like complete submission, because it leads directly to it.' *(Alexandre Guérin)*

Order and progression of rewards
- Allow the horse to act while no longer feeling the aids (descente des aides).
- Praise with hand or voice.
- Stop the exercise.
- Allow the horse some moments of rest.
- Give a treat.
- Return the horse to his stable.

This entire process is summarised by the illuminating formula of Faverot de Kerbrech, which is missing only one pre-condition: prepare carefully.

'Ask often, be content with a little and reward a lot.'

The seat

The rider's seat and posture, the very keystones of equitation, are interdependent.

The more deeply the rider sits, the better his posture will be, the torso raised and relaxed, legs hanging well down and adhering softly to the horse without gripping.'
(Nuno Oliveira)

'The posture is the first and last lesson the master learns … Everything becomes essential in an art in which little things make big differences.'
(Louis Charles Dupaty de Clam)

The seat is the 'mother' of all the aids, for various reasons:
- Without the ability to follow the horse's movement which comes from balance and suppleness, the rider cannot achieve the fixity in the saddle upon which the precision of the rein, leg and of course the weight aids depends. And nothing causes more trouble than the false fixity of the rider who grips with the legs and hangs on the horse's mouth.
- All good leg aids originate in the core, are transmitted through thigh and calf, extending if necessary to heel. In riding, the leg extends from the waist to the heel.
- Every effect of the hand begins with the play of the fingers on the reins, augmented if necessary by a rotation of the wrist fingernails upwards and including, if required, raising the hands (while the elbows remain close to the body without stiffness) … and, in the end, stretching up with the upper part of the body. One can say that in riding, the hand extends from the fingertips to the waist.
- Regardless of hand and leg, the seat also has its own effect; namely changes in the distribution of weight in the saddle as well as on the stirrups. The stirrups play the role of two scale pans, while the upper part of the body represents the beam of the scales.
- The active seat which 'pushes' in a certain direction encourages the horse to advance in this direction or, on the other hand, restricts movement in the opposite direction.
- The passive seat which weighs on the columns of support restricts the range of movement of the loaded legs and favours the range of motion of the unloaded legs.
- Since the rider's spine is so close to that of the horse, he perceives the movement and changes of balance through the play of his back.

Thus he feels the essential components of the gaits:
- the tempo, which describes the speed of movement in a certain gait;
- the rhythm, which characterises the gait (four, three or two beats) and which allows one to measure the frequency and regularity of the strides.
- The cadence, which reveals the expression and stylisation of a gait: its 'swing'. It originates from increased activity in the correct balance and results in bigger movements and extended suspension phases. The better the cadence, the more the rhythm slows. Although cadence appears in extensions, it is above all a characteristic of collected paces. The concept should not be devalued by using it indiscriminately.

The seat is also the 'child' of all the other aids. Combined, at first, in harmony with hand and leg, it gradually begins to substitute for them until in the end it is, so to speak, enough in itself.

'This means that the horse submits and balances himself little by little, until trained to work as if all by himself without the constant intervention of the aids.' *(Nuno Oliveira)*

The rein aids

Bringing the horse into hand (in French: mise en main) is by far the most complex and most controversial equestrian concept. It establishes impenetrable demarcation lines between the different schools of thought, while obedience to the leg aids (horse in front of the leg), apart from a few nuances, meets with general consensus.

Mise en main

The French concept, mise en main, literally means 'bringing into hand'. It describes the process in which the horse learns to become light to the hand, yield the mouth and flex at the poll, until he is eventually correctly 'on the bit' with a flexed poll and supple lower jaw, the nose slightly in front of or at the vertical and the poll remaining the highest point.

The 'wonder rider', Étienne Beudant, called his last book 'Hand without legs' … by that he wanted to express that 'a good hand can do everything'. Hence, it seems justified to regard the use of the hand as the primary aid.

To avoid any dogmatism, it is advisable to tackle such a subject by observation. So then, let us try to establish some principles by working step-by-step from facts which we know from experience.

If we remember that longitudinal flexibility stems from lateral flexibility, then the principles of gymnastics and biomechanics tell us that the rider's first job must be to stretch the top line, by bending and extending the neck. The first challenge he will face, in terms of gymnastics and elementary steering, will be to find a way of conveniently establishing the lateral bend of the neck.

But what does one hear over and over again about a horse that cannot be bent, for example, to the right?

'He is stiff on the right.'

This is a faulty analysis, in two ways:

- The same horse which stubbornly resists the toughest treatment with the sharpest tools can scratch his flank with his teeth without any trouble at all, with his neck bent about 180 degrees! The problem is not stiffness, but tension. Conclusion: the horse that is 'bracing' rather than 'stiff' is in much more need of 'relaxation' than 'gymnastics'.
- If the horse refuses to bend right, he 'defends himself' against the effect of the right rein … But the origin of this opposition is on the left side of the neck, where the muscles do not allow the stretch.

Secondly, one often hears the following judgment:

'He doesn't want to …'

An equally dubious explanation:

- If one stands next to the horse's shoulder, a light pressure of the hand on the left side of the horse's face is enough to have the horse turn his head clearly and without difficulty to the right.
- The old masters knew this, because they always began the education with reins fixed to a cavesson as a precaution. And isn't the use of the hackamore in modern day sport riding also a means to avoid provoking defences in the mouth?

Certainly, 'the horse only does well what he does with pleasure'(Charles-Hubert Raabe). But he never opposes without reason. In the case above, this reason lies in the mouth.

As a last resort, one reaches for the assertion that

'He has a hard mouth …'.

Now at first glance, how could one argue? However:

- The bit works on the tongue, which consists of mucous membrane; a tissue very richly supplied with blood, with nerves woven throughout its fabric – and which is, therefore, especially sensitive. Only someone who takes pleasure in biting his own tongue could argue! This is no different for the horse.

Clearly, this means that it is not that the mouth is hard, but that the bit attacks the tongue. Instinctively the horse tries to escape the pain caused with all his means:

- François Baucher expresses it brilliantly:

'There are no spoilt mouths just as there are neither hard nor soft mouths: all these concepts have no sense … Let us destroy this much too widespread mistake and replace "hard mouthed" with "hard to the hand" … The manufacturers of saddles and bridles have taken advantage of the ignorance or superficiality of most riders to change the shapes of bits and make them of a size which turns out almost always injurious for the horse and prevents the very effect one expects them to have.'

It is indeed easier to change the bit than the hand. The profusion of different bits and auxiliary reins available underlines only a crying helplessness, hiding an admission of helplessness under excessive complexity and an appearance of high technology. One could say in jest: 'The smaller the trainer's cupboard, the greater his knowledge.'

For the most part, 'defences' are no more than various means of 'rejection' of the foreign body in the mouth. The list is long, dependent on the temperament of the horse and the gravity of the mistakes committed by the rider:

- tension in the jaw, teeth tightly clenched;
- grinding the teeth;
- twisting at the poll;
- overflexed horse, behind the bit;
- stargazing, nodding or tugging against the hand;
- tongue held up, held out to the side or pulled over the bit;
- at the height of desperation the horse can become restive, in the end refusing to go forward, or even rearing;
- and which rider has not had the experience that even the horse that is hardest against the hand suddenly becomes submissive and permeable … just so long as he chews and swallows a treat?

The horse was not born with iron in his mouth. The fact that he feels uncomfortable and braces is natural. To avoid the phenomenon of rejection, the 'implant' must be accepted. The hand must educate the mouth, so that it accepts the foreign body and comes to play with it, instead of fearing it and trying to flee.

Some have tried hard to perfect bits that cause the jaw to yield and stimulate the natural play of the tongue, recognising that its mobility is a sign of légèreté and submission. Let's consider some of these tricky inventions in two categories.
• Negative: all kinds of 'tongue fixer', which sit behind the bit and prevent the horse from getting his tongue over it.
• Positive: the 'mastigadour': a kind of snaffle, decorated with small pieces of chain and other dangly items which the old masters used to stimulate mastication. The 'bits with toys' are only modern variations of the same principle.

But all these methods are only stopgaps, J. Pellier judges:

'I repeat again that mechanical aids cannot remove the bad habits of an animal and that only an educated and intelligent hand can give the horse the mobility of the jaw and the right posture of the head.'

Summary

Rein tension → pressure of the mouthpiece on the tongue → pain → tension and blocking of the lower jaw → by transference: spreading of these tensions to the muscles of the neck or the back etc.

Properly understood, the problem must be formulated as follows: how does one place the horse's head, using interventions of the hand which spare the tongue and are capable of relaxing the mouth by mobilising the jaw?

Baucher's second manner provides the principle on which the answer is based: instead of forcing a posture while squeezing the tongue and violating the mouth, begin by relaxing and educating it, while mobilising the jaw, by means of raising the hand.

Effects of raising the hand

Begin with correctly adjusted reins; that is to say, just enough tension to enable one to feel the mouth, because any stronger pressure would provoke unwanted muscle contractions.

Augment the tension of the right rein slowly by closing the fingers, rotating the wrist – fingernails upwards – and raising the hand. Because it approaches the longitudinal axis of the horse's head, the effect acts only on the corners of the mouth and not at all on the tongue (fig. 16 A). The left rein maintains contact.

Through the application of 'slow force', the tension of the rein is gradually increased, until the horse releases the lower jaw. This happens without fail, because raising the snaffle in the mouth triggers a swallowing reflex. If the rider yields immediately by opening the fingers, the horse is free to mobilise his lower jaw and tongue:

'This latter "slow and smooth" movement causes the parotid glands to emerge from their position, provoking a light salivation, the tongue raises the bit (or both bits) to the back of the mouth, letting them fall again as it returns to its normal resting place between the jaws. As they fall back into place the bits may collide and one hears the characteristic "clicking".' *(General Decarpentry)*

This is the basic 'yielding of the jaw' which relaxes the horse and in so doing disarms every defence against the hand. The old masters said that the horse 'savours the bit'.

Once the horse has shown his 'responsiveness to the hand' in this way, the rider can extend his raising of the right rein to bend the neck. So long as the horse yields his lower jaw, he will accept the increase of the lateral bend, provided the left rein does not oppose but merely limits it (fig. 16 B).

The bend can be increased bit by bit, until reaching the point where lateral bend and inversion of the neck are incompatible (90 degrees, if necessary). At this point, the horse will respond with a direct flexion at the poll. The rider answers with a release of the aid (descente de main):

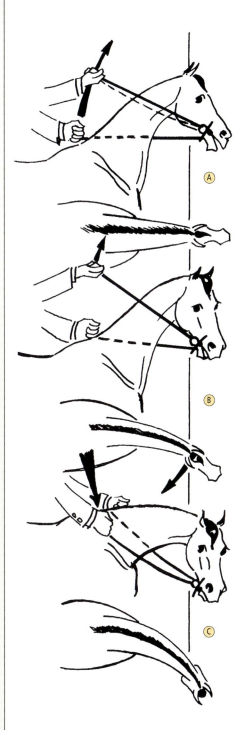

Fig. 16

Bending and stretching through an upwards-acting effect of the hand
Ⓐ *Yielding of the jaw*
Ⓑ *Sideways bending*
Ⓒ *Stretching of the neck due to bending*

a lowering of the right hand to 'half-tense' reins. By releasing the reins to a greater or lesser degree, the rider can determine the desired amount by which the neck stretches and extends.

In summary
Raising the inside rein → yielding of the lower jaw → lateral bend of the neck → yielding at the poll → soft connection in the outside rein and lowering of the hand holding the inside rein.

Division of the roles:
- Inside rein: asks for the yielding of the lower jaw and the lateral bend.
- Outside rein: regulates the bend and controls the degree of 'ramener' and the stretching of the neck.

This leads to the conclusion that, if the inside rein is used correctly, the outside rein takes over the primary role. It is barely surprising that this method is the precise opposite of the worst mistake: forcing the bend by pulling or fixing the inside rein, while the outside rein is left sagging.

Begun if necessary at the halt, or with extremely tense horses even from the ground, the practice is explained systematically on both reins, first at the walk, then at a trot and finally at the canter.

Thus one achieves the first, elementary bringing into hand: with a long, arched neck, the horse's face approximately vertical, a supple lower jaw and the mouthpiece acting softly on a relaxed tongue (fig. 16 C).

Which principles follow from this?
- In this order, the horse must yield only the lower jaw, then bend the neck to the side, the finally flex at the poll. In layman's terms, it must 'say yes' before 'nodding his head'.
- This leads to the rejection ipso facto of nosebands especially designed to keep the mouth closed. They are very much in fashion with dressage riders – while the regulations should actually forbid them.
- This leads also to the outright condemnation of overflexed, 'Rollkured' horses: the line of the nose behind the vertical with a dead mouth. Here, in effect, the horse bows his head 'yes' excessively to escape the hand while saying 'no' with his mouth. It is not 'brought into hand', it is 'behind the bit'. This should be considered as a defence.
- One should not confuse the overflexed horse with the practice of 'ramener outré', however; a short-lived, artificial, excessive ramener requested by the rider which is justified by certain conformational difficulties. This involves bringing the nose line temporarily behind the vertical, only after and with the continuing accompaniment of the yielding of the lower jaw.
- Leaning on the hand is not allowed, because the continual pressure which the snaffle (and the curb even more so) puts on the tongue cuts off the circulation. If the blood supply is interrupted, the tongue loses its sensitivity, which makes the horse harder in the hand, etc. – a vicious circle.

The rider must not confuse leaning on the hand with rein contact, just as he must not confuse légèreté with refusing the rein contact.

Initially, one must correct a horse that leans on the hand by the application of demi-arrêts (firm and lively movements of the hand from below to above), so that it comes off the hand and is inspired to carry itself in order to have then the possibility of yielding the lower jaw.

With a horse, however, that comes above the bit and refuses the contact with the rider's hand it is useful to clearly stretch the neck (by significant lateral bending) to encourage it to take an honest, steady connection.

- The 'fixed' hand and 'mise en main'
One cannot 'fix' the horse's head by fixing the hands to the withers.

The hand must be 'fixed' first of all in relation to the horse's mouth, which means it must accompany with suppleness all the natural movements of the head. Respect for the mouth and the yielding of the lower jaw depend on this. The hand may on no account restrain or even limit, but only act upwards to achieve the yielding of the jaw. In contrast to any attempt at compulsion, this raising of the hand is an aid as well as an indispensable precondition for the lowering of the hand and release of the rein (descente de main).

With the help of relaxation and with an increasingly stable posture of head and neck, the hand becomes gradually more and more 'fixed' in relation to the withers. Combining the activity of the haunches with mobility of the mouth, the perfection of the 'mise en main' depends on the elevation of the head and neck and the flexion at the poll: in other words, on the degree of 'ramener'.

Then finally, a 'fixed' hand with mobile fingers is sufficient, corresponding to a 'fixed' head with a supple jaw. The procedure cannot be reversed without violating the principles outlined above.

In conclusion
All of the above merely confirms and illustrates General L'Hotte's brilliant statement – corresponding to the 'last teachings' of François Baucher:

Demi-arrêt

The literal translation of the French term demi-arrêt is 'half-halt'. In the original sense, however, this did not mean the increased constriction between leg, seat and rein aids commonly used today but a pure effect of the hand acting from below to above. To distinguish between these meanings clearly, the French concept demi-arrêt is used throughout this book.

> ### Ramener
>
> The French concept, ramener, cannot be fully translated into English. The concept involves not only a flexion at the poll (the horse 'accepts the bridle') but also describes the posture of a horse completely on the aids that has firstly an elevated neck, secondly yields the mouth and then thirdly flexes at the poll in such a manner that the nose is slightly in front of or at the vertical and the poll remains the highest point.

'Bringing the horse into hand [ramener], such as it is understood in High School work, does not concentrate upon the posture of the head. It lies first of all in the submission of the jaw, the first spring which receives the effect of the hand. If this spring reacts with suppleness to the effect that stimulates its action, it encourages the flexibility of the neck and the pliability of the other springs …'

To sum up, one could say that the behaviour of the hand is symptomatic of two different conceptions of equitation: those who 'hold the head' and those who 'dialogue with the mouth'. Two irreconcilable philosophies which require one to choose the side of the fence on which one elects to sit.

Flexions in-hand

We owe the concept of flexions performed in-hand to François Baucher. His pupils and he himself applied them systematically and required extreme postures that were not always in harmony with the horse's conformation. This allowed his opponents to reject these exercises out of hand. There is no denying their fundamental usefulness, however.

Of course the horse must be relaxed and gymnasticised in his totality; however, the mouth is and remains the gateway that leads to these goals, and one needs the keys to the castle, since one cannot burgle one's way into a friend's house.

Teaching the rein aids in-hand
- is only useful for riders who have a correct understanding of a horse 'mise en main' (see 'The rein aids', p. 66) and who aim for légèreté (lightness);
- enables the preliminary education of the horse to the curb as well as a rational application of four reins;
- is of incomparable effectiveness with horses of unfavourable conformation and those which have been spoiled by bad hands. In these cases, conducting the introduction phase in-hand is a gentler and more effective starting point for re-education; in other words it is more intelligent than the application of various auxiliary reins;
- is really only worth doing if the rider's aids from the saddle build on the results achieved in-hand.

Principles
- Work primarily towards relaxation, while developing the mobility of the lower jaw and tongue, so that the horse contentedly savours his bit.
- Use this permeability to the rein aids to achieve a gymnastic development that leads to all useful postures. Lateral bending of the neck leads to flexion at the poll by stretching of the neck. Gradual closing of the angle at the poll results from subsequent elevation of the neck.
- Indirectly, via clearly distinguished posture changes, teach the effects of the different bits.
- Check that the yielding of the jaw can be obtained in every posture and in forward motion, at least in the walk, to be able to repeat them from the saddle.

The most important flexions
The most effective flexions are summarised below. The order cannot be changed, because the horse must be educated progressively: to yield the lower jaw, then learn the lateral flexions of the neck before, finally, flexing at the poll.

1. Yielding of the jaw on the snaffle
- (Fig. 17 A) With horses that lean on the bit because of a heavy, deeply set neck or bad education, but also with those which overflex: one can begin to show them a way out from this dead end by restoring a correct contact with the rider's hand in a natural posture.

Standing in front of the horse with thumbs in the snaffle rings, act with small movements, jerky if necessary, on the corners of the mouth in the direction of horse's ears. Lower the hands (descente de main) and praise, as soon as the horse carries his own head and mobilises his mouth. Draw the horse forwards a few steps and then begin the same action from in front. Thus the horse learns to move and halt without leaning on the bit or overflexing.

Once this procedure is successful one can tackle the next, but don't hesitate to go back a step if necessary.
- (Fig. 17 B) With horses that go above the bit, the technique must be immediately adjusted as follows:

standing next to the head, lay the outside rein over the poll. Act on the reins by bringing the hands towards one another. Acting in this manner, raise the snaffle in the mouth until the horse clearly opens his lower jaw. Release and allow the horse to play with the mouthpiece. One can encourage this with vibration. Praise, advance and repeat.

2. Yielding of the jaw on the curb
- By a crossover effect: at the same time draw the snaffle rein upward and the opposite curb rein towards the rear.
- (Fig. 17 C) With all four reins: in combination, draw both curb reins to the back and both snaffle

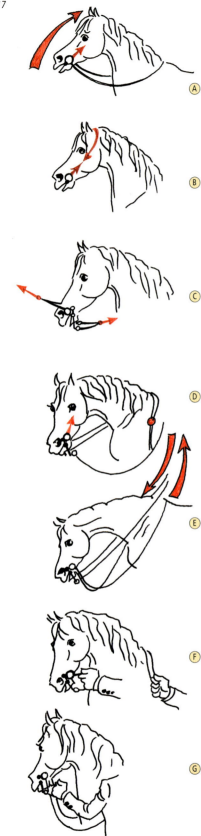

Fig. 17

The principal flexions on the snaffle and curb

reins forwards (after one has passed them under the branches of the curb). Bring the horse forward with the snaffle reins. Praise. Thus the horse learns not to fear the curb and to give his mouth without lowering at the poll – instead of resisting at the poll with clenched teeth. This is also an extremely effective means to correct an inclination toward overflexing.

3. Lateral flexion of the neck

(Fig. 17 D) Obtain the release of the jaw, then a lateral flexion of the neck by raising the inside snaffle rein while retaining the connection with the outside snaffle and curb reins. Bend the neck until the horse lengthens it.

Come forward on a curve. Praise. The horse learns in this order: yield the jaw, bend the neck and, finally, yield at the poll. This is the precise opposite of the method that leads to overflexion: flexion at the poll without any real lateral suppleness and with resistance in the lower jaw.

4. Extension of the neck on the curb

(Fig. 17 E) Pass the outside rein over the poll. Act upwards with both curb reins until obtaining the release of the jaw, then flexion at the poll and, finally, stretching of the neck.

Put the horse in the desired posture. Walk forwards. Praise.

Thus, the horse learns to flex at the poll in order to stretch its neck and the curb takes on the role of 'neck extender' and becomes the antidote against overflexing and false lightness.

5. With all four reins

(Fig. 17 F) Once the horse understands and can do the following:

- yield the lower jaw in response to the snaffle or curb and savour the bits;
- that the snaffle elevates the head, opens the angle between head and neck and provokes lateral bending of the neck;
- that the curb is used to cause flexion at the poll and extension of the neck;

now – one can take up all four reins to combine their effects with the play of the fingers and wrists.

It is easy to see that these exercises can only be developed further by holding the reins in the so-called 'French manner' (à la française, also widely known as the 'Fillis method').

6. Working on the curb alone

(Fig. 17 G) If the mise en main is developed far enough, in the end the horse can be worked from the ground only on the curb with the reins held crossed in one hand behind the chin groove. The horse can be elevated to any degree. The other hand is free to use the schooling whip.

If one already has some experience, one can achieve significant results with these procedures even in the first few lessons and even in the most difficult cases. As a precondition, however, it is assumed that one is not content with a crude conception of a horse on the aids.

Selection and use of bits

Selection

As we all know, the intelligent use of the hand spares the rider from having recourse to a whole arsenal of bits and auxiliary reins, each more complex and more severe than the other. The right bit is that which corresponds best of all to the shape of the mouth and which rests on the bars and tongue while respecting the latter as much as possible.

Snaffle

Avoid mouthpieces that are too thick and which needlessly take up a lot of space in the mouth – as well as ones that are too thin and which cut in.

The width of the bit should be selected according to the horse's jaw, so that it does not slide to and fro in the mouth.

Choose rings that hold the bit quiet in the mouth and lie close at the sides without pressing. From this point of view the D-ring snaffle and the Fulmer-cheeked snaffle are particularly effective.

Curb

As a leverage bit, the curb can only work backwards, its power being proportional to the length of the branches and the adjustment of the curb chain.

The bars are by nature less sensitive than the tongue. The mouthpiece must therefore be adapted to the cross section of the mouth, so that it lies on the bars in order that the pressure on the tongue is reduced and its free mobility is not hindered. It follows, then, that a 'port' corresponding to the thickness of the tongue reduces the effect of the curb instead of sharpening it, as is so often heard.

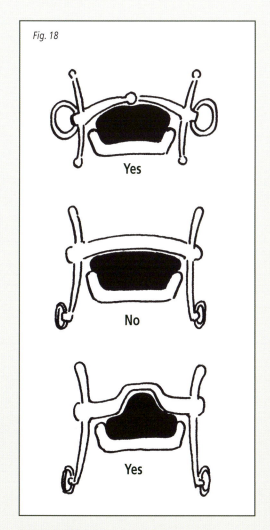

Effects of different shaped bits on the tongue and bars

Use

Depending on the position of the hand, the snaffle can have an effect on the corners of the mouth or on the tongue – while the curb, whatever one does with it, always on works on the bars and tongue. There is general agreement, therefore, that the snaffle is used for stretching and elevation, the curb, in contrast, for flexing and lowering. On condition, of course, that the mouth responds willingly …

Holding the reins

On a fully trained horse that is perfectly light, the rider holds the reins however he chooses – then the horse can be ridden even on the curb alone with the reins in one hand. This, anyway, was the objective towards which the old masters worked, for reasons of elegance as well as effectiveness.

One should not confuse the goal and the means, however.

The associated use of two bits makes sense only if one has the possibility of separating their effects whenever one chooses, so as later to be able to combine them according to one's needs.

'Since the snaffle sits higher in the mouth than the curb, its principal effect lies in raising the horse's head, while the curb, more than anything else, lowers it. All schools agree on these basic points. In other words, the snaffle elevates, the curb lowers. It appears, and it is even certain that the snaffle and the curb reins must be held in similar fashion to the places that the snaffle and curb occupy in the mouth, that is to say, the former above the latter … Reason demands that the reins are held in French manner.'
(James Fillis, *Principes de dressage et d'équitation*, 1890)

Unfortunately, this French manner of holding the reins is very little known and is used even less – without doubt because 'it's hard to be a prophet in one's own land'. As Fillis noted: 'Isn't it strange that the French army follows the German army regulations, with the snaffle reins below the curb?'

Holding the reins 'à la française'

The way in which the reins are held is by no means a trivial matter; it must not be considered simply some fashion phenomenon, but must be carefully studied and considered.

Holding the reins à la française originated with the old masters who, in order to separate the raising and lowering effects, held the reins of the cavesson in one hand (held higher) and the curb reins in the other (held lower). When the full double bridle (combination of snaffle and curb) came into general use, several of the best écuyers continued to use this approach. Many pictures prove it, albeit with some idiosyncrasies which, however, do not call the principle into question.

An écuyer of English origin, James Fillis, praised the merits of this method very highly. Despite having the emphatic support of the future President Clemenceau, Fillis did not succeed in being accepted into the Cadre Noir, eventually becoming Écuyer en chef in Saint Petersburg. There he continued to transmit this approach to Russian riders: snaffle rein between thumb and forefinger, curb rein under the little finger. In the 1960s and 1970s the Soviet dressage team, who had stuck with this method of holding the reins, won numerous international competitions.

Nuno Oliveira, an advocate of equitation in the French tradition, also chose to hold the reins this way, and nobody will deny that his horses were especially light.

This method is a logical step for légèreté. Indeed, for anyone who accepts, after L'Hotte and therefore Baucher, that the mobility of the jaw dominates and causes suppleness of the neck, it is only natural to separate the diametrically opposite effects of the snaffle and curb, in order to be able afterwards to consciously combine their complementary effects.

With supple play of his fingers and wrists, the rider can vary the effect on the horse's posture with the greatest possible precision and quickness.

At will, in a fraction of a second, he can:
- establish contact on one, two, three or four reins;

- intervene with the snaffle alone to achieve de-contraction, bending, raising, légèreté;
- apply the curb alone to flex at the poll or to extend the neck;
- make use of 'divided support' by combining the snaffle on one side with the curb on the other side;
- and finally, manage his horse on all four reins or on the curb alone, as soon as it goes correctly and is light.

Progression for teaching the mise en main with the curb

Whether training a young horse correctly prepared on the snaffle, or re-educating a horse spoiled by bad hands, the work is always based on the same basic principles: the judicious application of the reins held à la française allows the rider to produce all kinds of effects from the saddle.

In other words, it is the faithful continuation of the flexions in-hand, to which one can always return, but which become practically superfluous. From the saddle, the rider has, in effect, from the outset the possibility of developing an association between 'yielding of the jaw' and 'impulsion', while flexions in-hand are necessarily static and, therefore, of limited use.

Through the yielding of the jaw, the horse must learn bit by bit that the snaffle signifies 'elevation, extension', while the curb means 'flexion, lowering'. The snaffle is always primary, because only it can spare the tongue since its effect acts upwards on the corner of the lips. Thus it provokes the yielding of the jaw, by which means the horse is brought to accept the contact of the curb, which works by force of leverage only on the tongue and, whether one wishes it or not, towards the rear. And so the horse comes little by little to an understanding of the curb effect with a supple mouth, instead of resisting or overflexing.

Each of the following learning steps must be begun with the yielding of the jaw and be finished with lowering of the hand and release of the rein (descente de main). In this way the horse finds his reward – and the rider the proof of having performed his work correctly.

As the precision of the understanding increases, the rider's aids become more discreet, the horse's reactions faster and more durable. In the end, tiny variations of the rein contact are enough to induce the desired responses.

Phase A Initial yielding of the jaw

By a gradual, slowly increasing, upwards tension of the snaffle reins (which can even become a demi-arrêt in the case where a horse is leaning on the bit) the rider raises the horse's neck up to the

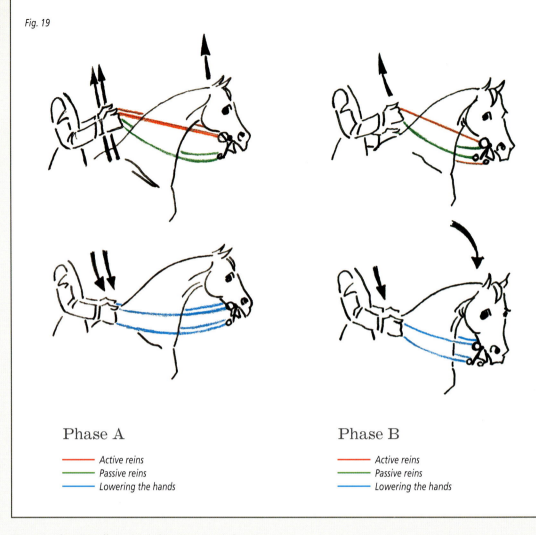

Fig. 19

Phase A
— Active reins
— Passive reins
— Lowering the hands

Phase B
— Active reins
— Passive reins
— Lowering the hands

The range of possible effects while holding the reins à la française

Reins à la française

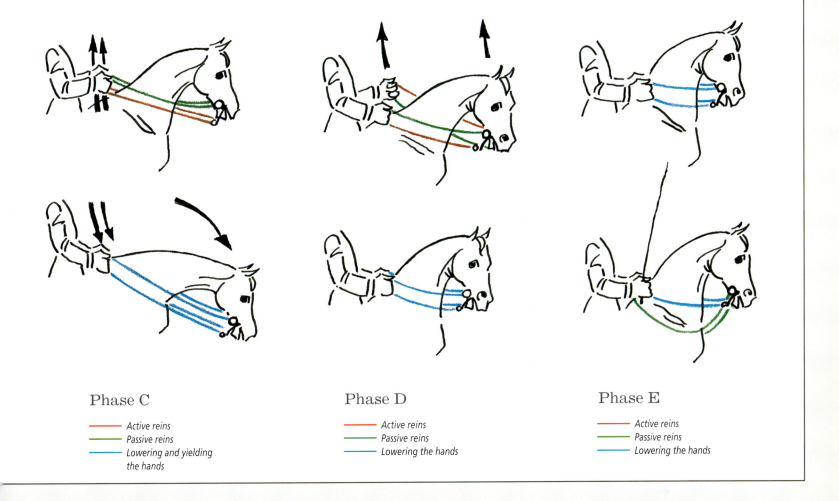

Phase C
— Active reins
— Passive reins
— Lowering and yielding the hands

Phase D
— Active reins
— Passive reins
— Lowering the hands

Phase E
— Active reins
— Passive reins
— Lowering the hands

point where the latter carries his head himself and opens his mouth slightly. Lower the hands, as long as the horse mobilises his jaw and savours the bit without changing his posture. Begin again so often as necessary to reawaken an immobile, dead mouth.

Phase B Lateral bending of the neck and flexion at the poll
By raising the inside snaffle rein and limiting with the outside curb rein: obtain a yielding of the jaw and increase the lateral bend of the neck until this provokes a yielding at the poll. Bending alternately on both sides, the horse becomes round and, in addition, seeks the contact in the outside curb rein while giving the mouth. This is the best weapon against an inverted neck.

Phase C Extension of the neck
On gently raising both curb reins, the horse must respond by mobilising his jaw, then accompany the rider's lowering and advancing hands by rounding and extending his neck. The horse follows the bits until the desired point, then pauses there and savours the mouthpiece. With this practice, during which the horse may neither pull, nor refuse the contact, the rider has at his disposal the best antidote against overflexion.

Phase D Elevation of the neck
With a suppled jaw and neck, the horse can be encouraged to elevate little by little and to increase the degree of flexion at his poll. The inside curb rein establishes the lateral bend, while demi-arrêts on the outside snaffle rein initiate the raising of the neck. Little by little the horse grows taller and remains in-hand, some of the time bent one way, some of the time the other.

Phase E The complete mise en main
Via alternate small effects with the snaffle or the curb, the rider can ask for more self-carriage and ramener. Gradually the horse reaches the ideal posture: base of the neck elevated as much as possible, with complete yielding at the poll and mobility of the jaw. In the end, the horse can be ridden in total légèreté on the curb alone with one hand. At least this was the aim of the old masters.

Reducing the component of skill, which is inevitably personal and not very transmissible, in favour of a methodical way of working, this way of holding the reins has an undeniable educational value. In other words, it is as worthwhile for the education and preservation of the horse as for the training of the rider.

All those whom I have had the opportunity to help understand this method have afterwards confessed they could no longer continue without it. Some people presumed to try to forbid me from using this method in my work with my own horses, without justification and even though they had admittedly never even tried it out – it takes all sorts!

If this method is properly understood, it also allows one to answer, with more than truisms, the famous question: 'From which point can a horse can be worked on the curb?'

- If it is a question of resorting to the curb to force a ramener which the rider cannot obtain on the snaffle alone through mobilisation of the jaw: then it is still too early, even if the horse is twenty years old.
- If it is a matter of separating the effects of snaffle and curb and then combining them in a logical manner to improve the mobilisation of the jaw before developing the ramener: then it is never too early, even if the horse is only four years old.

It is unreasonable to condemn the curb in itself as sharp, rather than the way the rider uses it. A torture instrument in the hand of one rider, it can be a source of relaxation in the hand of another.

'A horse that is worked through the mouth can be ridden with the light touch of the finger tips on the rein, while one that is worked by the neck needs constant tension in the arms and reins. That is why the former type of equitation is all about delicacy, the latter all about strength.'
(James Fillis)

The role of the hand

Numerous texts have tried to assign a more or less complex nomenclature of the 'rein effects' with the principal result of reinforcing a 'mechanical' and 'scholarly' way of riding, which became the norm for riding instructors and examiners. Their positive consequences for the education of horses still remain to be proven since, as ethical researcher Boris Cyrulnik wrote: 'Mechanical animals have been rusty for a long time.'

Even the very concept of 'effects' puts excessive focus on the results, while forgetting the horse and his indispensable education, which is actually the whole point of the matter. In reality the problem is much more simple, but much less simplistic.

If one takes into consideration the priorities explained above as well as the chronology of the education of the horse, one must conclude that the hand must first of all relax, then position and then, finally, guide the horse.

The relaxing hand

As a precondition for every correct effect, the hand must test the permeability of the mouth by soliciting the mobilisation of the jaw: the horse savours his bit without changing the posture of his head. Obtained at first by a raising of the snaffle reins acting on the corners of the mouth, the mobilisation of the jaw is achieved in the end, just through the play of the fingers, at first on the snaffle, then on the curb reins.

'Resistances of weight' (Baucher)
If the horse leans on the bit, the rider corrects with demi-arrêts in order that the horse 'unsticks' his mouth from the bit and raises his neck up to the point where it carries itself and he can give his mouth again.

'Resistances of force' (Baucher)
If the horse opposes a certain posture with a dead, immobile mouth, the rider tries first to restore the dialog by rapid vibration of the reins. If this does not succeed, he returns to the basic yielding of the jaw.

'If, when attempting some new movement, the mobility of the horse's jaw should be reduced, the first concern of the educated rider is to regain it as soon as possible.' (L'Hotte)

The 'positioning' hand
The horse which gives his mouth allows his rider to modify at will the attitude of his unified balancing rod and steering apparatus – the head and neck. If one understands the ways in which posture influences balance and movement, one can only agree with François Baucher's famous formula:

'Position precedes action.'

Bending
That is, to give the appropriate incurvation for the full range of lateral suppling exercises. At first raising the inside snaffle is necessary. In the end, merely the play of the fingers and wrists is enough.

Stretching
Elongates the top line and transfers weight to the forehand. In the beginning, the rider obtains the stretching of the neck by means of a suitable lateral bend which leads to flexion at the poll. In the end, the simple act of taking a frank 'contact' on the snaffle and above all on the curb (which lowers) and then 'giving' with the hand is sufficient to cause the horse to round his neck while stretching his head away from the shoulders without leaning on the bit or setting his mouth. Apart from its gymnastic benefit, the extension of the neck serves also as a complement, the antidote even, of demi-arrêts.

The guiding hand
In a commendable attempt at completeness, many authors recommend extremely complex combinations of the aids. This produces an excessively

interventionist way of riding in which the horse is like a puppet controlled by 'button pressure' and 'mechanics'.

But the better one 'does', the less one has to 'do':

'Instead of trying to match his effects to the movement of the horse's legs, the rider finds a substantially more interesting and more fertile field of application if he takes care of the perfection of position, that is, the combination of the forces and thereby the distribution of weight appropriate to every movement.'
(Alexis L'Hotte)

The more the horse gives his mouth and takes with ease the posture conducive to the desired movement, the less reason to apply force or even use the aids 'in opposition' which, by definition, impedes impulsion and balance.

To initiate a change of direction, the hand (in harmony with the other aids) may limit itself to altering the distribution of weight between the shoulders.

In this regard one must agree on a precise terminology:
- 'Inside – outside' refers to the bend of the horse: the inside aid corresponds to the hollow (concave) side, the outside aid to the convex side.
- 'Inner – outer' refers to the riding arena. 'Outer' signifies the side of the boundaries or fence, 'inner' the side toward which one moves.

There are two cases:

'True' bend:
Bent by the inside rein (the 'bending rein' according to the old masters) the horse moves in the direction of the bend due to the effect of the outside rein (the 'enveloping rein' according to the old masters) which causes a transfer of weight onto the inside shoulder.

This effect of the 'enveloping rein' is known in English as the 'indirect rein' (also known as 'neck rein' or 'supporting rein'); the rein on one side approaches the horse's neck and turns him away to the opposite side.

'Counter' bending:
In this case, the bend is initiated by the outer rein and limited by the inner rein. The horse moves in the opposite direction to the bend due to the effect of the 'inside' rein which causes a weight transfer onto the 'outside' shoulder (towards the inner side, in other words). The effect with the 'inside' rein is repeated or interrupted according to the desired movement and is lowered and released (descentes de main) as often as possible.

Consequences
By judicious use of the indirect rein, the rider may straighten his horse at any moment with more and more discretion and effectiveness by straightening the neck and replacing the horse's shoulders in front of his haunches.

Turning in true bend (above) and counter-bend (below)

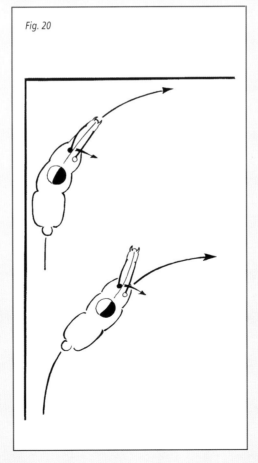

Fig. 20

Leg aids

'Often one hears that someone is an exceptional rider because he has very good hands. One seldom hears that another is a great rider because he uses his legs very well. Both are of equal importance for anyone who wants to be considered a good rider ... Submission and impulsion are two qualities that must be intimately connected in the education of the horse.' (Nuno Oliveira)

Impulsion

'This horse is light to the leg ... that horse lacks impulsion' are familiar statements which lead one to surmise that it is a matter of luck whether a horse obeys the legs well or not at all.

That is not at all the case, however, as General Decarpentry makes clear when speaking of the 'conquest of impulsion'. In fact, a horse that is lively when running free can appear resistant under the saddle, while one that looks quite placid at liberty can prove to be hypersensitive once mounted. Activity and reactivity must not, therefore, be confused. Impulsion arises from an education to the leg aids which have in themselves no inherent forwards-driving effect – spurs even less so.

Crouching on the back of the instinctively gregarious herbivore, which the horse is by nature, the rider finds himself actually in the position of a predator. The primordial fears linked with this explain how much starting a horse is a critical phase, in which clumsiness or brutality can leave indelible tracks. Developing the necessary trust requires a real 'taming' process, at the end of which the rider is accepted as a 'dominant congener'.

Depending on his temperament, the horse reacts to the aggression which the legs of the rider represent, either by freezing in tension or with violent defences. One should therefore consider impulsion as the expression of légèreté to the leg aids (the horse 'moves easily off the leg'). This is easily defined by the formula in Table 4.

Schwung and Impulsion

'Different languages use different terms to describe various qualities of forwards movement'

In German, the term Schwung is used, while in French and English one speaks of 'impulsion'. These terms are not identical, however. Schwung is above all a natural disposition, a consequence of breeding that one can buy. Impulsion, on the other hand, describes a high degree of responsiveness which is developed by educating the horse to the signals from the rider's leg. For those interested in dressage, it is therefore impulsion which is the determining factor.'

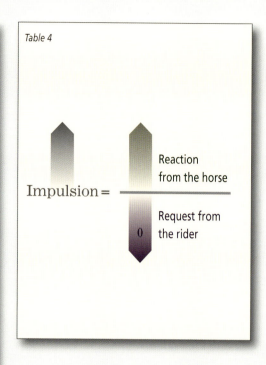

Table 4

It clearly shows that impulsion is directly proportionally to the energy with which the horse reacts (which is clear) – and inversely proportional to the intensity of the actions of the rider (which is much less obvious).

In fact, doesn't one hear everywhere: 'Push him forward – push your horse forward – use your legs – stronger! This is a big mistake for two reasons:

• Firstly, the words convey the wrong idea. Just as it is impossible to push a barrow one is sitting in, so a rider cannot 'push' a horse, for the very good reason that the rider is on top of the horse! Instead of pushing the horse, the rider can only 'ask' him to start moving himself – something totally different.

Everything depends, therefore, on the quality of education to the leg aids, which is the rider's responsibility. By the power of persuasion, the rider must achieve understanding and respect.

• Secondly, it is clear that a stronger action, even in order to increase the output, does nothing to improve the 'response to the leg' that is the definition of impulsion. If a certain degree of forwardness can be established with less use of the legs, however, that does indicate a higher degree of impulsion.

Let's conclude this discussion on obedience to the leg with two practical observations: one an educational matter, the other concerning competition.

• Riding instructors should not blunt their charges with more and more aids from legs and spurs, but should teach their pupils how they can educate their horses to the legs in an intelligent way.

• The principal justification of competition riding lies in its role as a test. It is illogical, then, if two horses performing a movement of comparable quality receive the same marks, if one rider sits quietly while the other is sweating away – the judges should take this into consideration in every single movement, not just in a collective mark at the end that has much too little influence on the result. Otherwise, good natural gaits are rewarded more than the horsemanship demonstrated, financial power more than skill. Thus one only discourages good riders who get the best out of modest horses: a heavy responsibility.

The conquest of impulsion

Principle

The only reliable factor that the rider can rely on to produce forward movement is the intelligent exploitation of the horse's natural flight instinct. In the beginning, anything unexpectedly entering his field of view causes a lively reaction.

By associating the pressure of his leg with a tap of the stick or whip behind the leg (adjusted according to the sensitivity of the horse and the effect desired), he makes himself understood. In this way he creates a conditioned response, the legs eventually substituting for the whip completely.

Method

'It is notable that a strike of the whip, if used in a just and timely manner, makes more impression and drives an indignant horse substantially better than pricking or tickling.'
(La Guérinière)

Use of the whip

• No tight or gripping legs, which would only blunt or suffocate the horse's natural sensitivity. Establish a contact of the legs that takes account of the sensitivity of the horse's skin. Hot-blooded, ticklish horses feel more secure when they are able to feel a frank and consistent contact of the rider's legs, which act with gradual pressure. In contrast, cold-blooded or lazy horses react better if the legs 'take them by surprise'; kept barely in contact then used in an insinuating, lively and electrifying way.

• Never be content if the application of the leg fails to elicit a frank and immediate reaction. Use the whip with enough energy to produce forward movement that is significantly more than the original requirement. For example: the rider asks for a transition from the walk to

the trot – the horse ignores the request – the whip sends the horse forward into the canter. Acting in this manner makes the alternative clear and there is no danger that the horse confuses request and reprimand.
- Do not oppose with the hand. Allow the forward movement to be expressed completely, even to excess. Reward, firstly by total release of the leg (descente de jambes), then by returning to calm: walk and praise. Then, after a short moment of reflection, repeat from the beginning as often as necessary – very little if it is done correctly.
- Spare the horse from any use of the leg so long as it advances. Constant use of the aids would serve only to make the horse dull and the legs ineffective. There is value in scarcity. In addition, should the horse slow down of his own initiative, do not correct him with the legs but rather with an appropriate intervention with the whip.
- The lazier the horse, or the more it holds back, the shorter and more energetic must be the periods of work, interspersed with moments of rest and praise. Repetition instructs, boredom destroys. One educates with persistence, not by wearing the horse down.

The application of this five-point programme enables one to stamp absolute obedience to the leg into the horse's psyche, which guarantees lasting, generous impulsion. The horse becomes alive to the 'draught of the boot'.

Observations

In dressage competitions one can often observe certain behaviour which is peculiar to this discipline and which betrays a questionable understanding of 'obedience to the leg': many riders retain their whips and relinquish them (as required by the regulations) only at the last moment before entering the arena. This approach is as much an admission of failure as it has become fashionable. It lies somewhere between terrible and laughable.

Really this practice takes little account of the horse's psychology in general and his memory in particular. If one wanted to teach the horse with the help of repetition that he is expected to behave himself outside the arena but not in the arena itself, one would not act any differently! It is compounding one error with another.

There is another much more subtle and intelligent way, one that the old masters were fond of – riding with the whip carried vertically. While the 'fashion police' see only someone posing in an outdated manner, it is actually a method that is extremely effective and elegant at the same time. Held in the upright position, the whip disappears from the horse's field of view, while at the same time the possibilities for its use are greatly increased. With the reins in one hand, the rider can touch wherever he judges it useful: on the shoulders, behind the leg, on the left or the right, on the croup, etc. – and the whip becomes a potential threat, as soon as it disappears from sight; intelligent and very effective. Horses that are accustomed to it redouble their energy as soon as the whip is moved to thisposition.

If one only takes the trouble to associate the whip with a very discreet click of the tongue, one will soon have a powerful means of admonition at one's disposal, without any of the undesirable side-effects of the whip (swishing of the tail, displacement of the hindquarters, raising of the croup etc.). If the teacher thinks, the pupil understands.

'Although the whip is more a matter of graceful appearance than necessity, one can take advantage of it whenever useful.' (La Guérinière)

Use of the spurs

'One must use them energetically and when required, but rarely, because nothing discourages and demeans a horse more than spurs used badly and too frequently.' *(La Guérinière)*

This means that spurs may serve merely to punish laziness or negligence, and consequently their use must be limited to the occasional extension of calf pressure, instead of tending to replace it.

This is even truer since the spurs have in themselves no inherent forwards-driving effect – in fact, the contrary. Most often, horses are inclined to hold back or even to stop in response to an 'attack with the spurs', especially since the latter will be sharp and the horse is sensitive by nature. With this in mind, the 'education to the spur' as recommended in Baucher's second manner and described by Faverot de Kerbrech is essential. It is carried out in two steps:
- The horse is 'introduced' to the spurs. One achieves this with a little patience by accustoming the horse to stand absolutely quietly while both spurs are frankly applied. Trust develops.
- Teach the meaning of the spurs. By increased pressure of the spurs, ride forwards at walk or in trot. Use the whip to help, if necessary, but immediately yield with the spurs and allow the horse to proceed in complete release of the legs (descente de jambes).

In this way one quickly teaches the horse to accept, understand and respect the spurs – instead of fearing and reacting to them with tension. The horse fears nothing more than the unknown.

Position of the legs

Effective use of the propulsive aids assumes that the rider's legs and spurs lie properly on the horse. There are many riders who, to 'do dressage', adjust their stirrups longer than their legs. This causes them to stand on tiptoe in the stirrups with their heels pulled up, and thus the spurs constantly in the fur. Hence, the horse is never aided by the legs, but is bothered constantly by the spurs. The teacher punishes his pupil without even having posed a question.

If, however, the rider adjusts his stirrups in such a way that his legs lie relaxed, well descended and enveloping the horse, with his ankles flexed and the heel a little lower than the toes (with quite short spurs, carried so that they are not in contact) – then he can use the propulsive aids with discernment:
- Ordinarily: pressure of the calf on the belly by lowering of the heel

- Exceptionally: call to order with the spurs by a brief turning out of the toes.

If one adds that the relaxed enveloping of the legs contributes substantially to firmness in the saddle, the rider can only benefit.

The effects of the legs

To be properly understood by the horse and to be able to use a broad range of indications, the rider must create a 'language of the legs' and codify their application with the greatest possible logic, precision and variety.

Conventions are only useful insofar as they are logical and consistent and the following criteria must be considered:

Position of the horse

When the horse is straight: the legs lie symmetrically.

When the horse is bent: the leg on the hollow side hangs below the rider (at the girth), the leg on the convex side is carried slightly further back (behind the girth).

When the horse is moving obliquely: for work on two tracks, the isolated or dominating effect of one leg must provoke a lateral movement of the hindquarters: the horse 'yields to the leg'. If the horse's body is incurved and the inside leg at the girth (hollow side) provokes a yielding of the haunches, one obtains the shoulder-in position. If, however, the outside leg placed behind the girth (on the convex side) requests it, one obtains the travers position.

Tempo

The equal pressure of both legs in their natural position (hanging plumb below the seat) must cause an immediate increase in speed. This sets the horse in forward motion.

The equal pressure of both legs behind their basic position must cause an increase in activity. This effect, depending on the other aids, can be produced without acceleration or even while slowing down the pace.

Because these aids have their effect near the horse's belly musculature, they stimulate the active stepping forward of the hindquarters under the body. They are related to collection.

Rhythm

The first duty of the legs is to stay 'fixed', which doesn't mean blocking or pinching, but going along softy with all movements of the trunk to maintain a light connection. Only under this condition can the legs of the rider accompany and have an effect on the rhythm, the frequency of the strides and therefore intervene in perfect harmony with the gait – to reinforce it, not jostle or hurry it.

Horses are like a metronome in two-, three- or four-beat rhythm. Every horse has his own natural rhythms in every gait, which one must respect above all else.

Cadence

If the legs are to obtain more impulsion, they may not act more 'strongly' (danger of dulling the horse), but more 'often': the horse responding significantly to every intervention. The movement becomes more 'cadenced' each time the increase in activity is connected with a slowing down of the rhythm. The horse develops 'expression'. There are two situations:
- The horse accelerates, not through taking short strides with increased frequency (hurrying), but through taking very long strides. The suspension phase becomes longer and the rhythm slows. Horizontal projection increases: extension.
- The horse's action increases without accelerating or even while slowing the pace, while the strides become more elevated and show more rebound. The suspension phase becomes longer and the rhythm slows. Vertical projection increases: collection.

A slower rhythm with sluggish hindquarters may not be regarded as cadence, because it is the result of laziness.

In the ideal case one reaches a stage where one no longer knows whether it is the rider's aids that stimulate the horse, or whether his flanks rhythmically draw in and push off the legs of the rider.

The effet d'ensemble

We owe the effet d'ensemble (in English: combined effect) whose 'effect' is assured, by the way, only after progressive preparation, to the brilliant innovator François Baucher.

It constitutes an infallible means of domination that is without doubt helpful, even indispensable, with certain horses – namely those which often try to evade the rider on account of poor conformation, a difficult character or a very quick temper.

Principles

In principle, the effet d'ensemble allows the rider to dissolve all resistances and put the horse on the aids once again. It is the 'call to attention' of equitation – and the écuyer's 'secret weapon':

'A clear and energetic pressure of the spurs sets the horse against the bit which forms a barrier until the achievement of immobility or the restoration of regular steps if one is in movement.'
(René Bacharach)

'Once légèreté reappears, one releases first the fingers, then the spurs and lastly the legs. The effet d'ensemble practised in this way without hesitation is the only absolutely sure way to prevent a resistance.' (Faverot de Kerbrech)

Limitations

As the starting point of education in Baucher's 'first manner', the effet d'ensemble has provoked numerous controversies and much opposition. Indeed, it required all the master's skill to avoid totally suffocating impulsion and, besides – 'not everyone is Baucher'.

The application which Baucher's second manner suggests is much more accessible in comparison, because here the effet d'ensemble arises from the attention to the principle 'hand without legs, legs without hand'. The big question is: how can one ensure that the powerful instrument of domination does not contravene this wise principle?

Preconditions

Some precautions are necessary to ensure that the forwards-driving potential of the leg aids is in no way impaired.

Essential conditions for the teaching of the effet d'ensemble:
• The horse goes forward from the 'draught of the boot'.
• The horse yields the jaw and extends his neck correctly.
• The horse has been carefully educated to the spurs

Method

The use of the effet d'ensemble no longer presents any risk if clear differentiations are made, namely in relation to: the interplay of the aids, the position of the legs and the application of the spurs.

Sending the horse forwards:
• No opposition from hand or seat (legs without hand).
• Legs hanging below the seat.
• Brief pressure from the legs. Exceptionally lively, brief 'attack' with the spurs. Total release of the leg aids (descente de jambes) in forward movement.

The effet d'ensemble

• The upper body is carried back together with opposition from the hands which are 'fixed' with the fingers closed.
• The legs are placed in front of their normal position, on the girth.

• Steady, constant pressure of the legs, strengthened immediately by clear, increasing spur pressure directly at the girth – up to the complete immobilisation of the horse.

What happens?

Physiologically, a steady pressure of the spurs has a paralysing influence on the affected muscle groups. If the spurs are used near the girth and the sternum, they affect the pectoral muscles, the sternohyoid muscle (which runs from the sternum to the underside of the mouth) and, by transference, indirectly affect the humero-mastoid muscles. Sudden contraction of these muscles stops the movement of the forelegs, lowers the head, causes the horse to flex at the poll and mobilises the lower jaw.

These halts by the effet d'ensemble are practised at first from the walk, then obtained also from the trot and, finally, the canter. Quite quickly the rider obtains immediate halts, even from a strong gallop. As soon as the horse stands, thanks to the aids of the spurs, immobile and on the aids again, the rider must of course release or even give with the hands, then release the pressure of the spurs and, finally, the legs.

Additional precautions

Immediately after every successful effet d'ensemble, ask for an instantaneous return to an energetic trot or canter simply by returning the legs to their initial position. Bit by bit the horse memorises the following: 'Forward movement always has the last word. Effet d'ensemble = stop, then begin again with more sparkle.'

Far from damaging impulsion, the effet d'ensemble performed in this manner contributes efficiently towards its improvement.

Perfection

Through careful repetition of the same practice – pressure of the calves, extended by that of the spurs – there comes a time when the horse immobilises on closing the lower legs at the girth, even before the spurs so much as touch the hair. Naturally the rider will dispense with their application, thus rewarding this gratifying anticipation – which must now only be repeated and refined. Thereafter the rider only returns to the spurs to refresh the horse's memory in case of disobedience.

When the horse responds well to halts by the effet d'ensemble, it becomes possible to use it to obtain complete yielding in every gait: first at the walk, then at the trot and finally at the canter. If the rider applies the effet d'ensemble progressively without first leaning back with the upper part of the body, the horse reacts by going back on the aids without thinking of stopping or even slowing.

It is a question of the harmony and dosage of the aids, certainly delicate, but within the capabilities of any rider with an independent seat and a horse that is correctly prepared.

The main principle that governs any intelligent use of the aids also applies, of course, to the effet d'ensemble: use it as sparingly as possible so as not to dilute its effect. One should also use it with the aim of refining the horse's reaction through progressively more and more economical application.

Notes

Not all horses justify resorting to the effet d'ensemble, but some never submit completely without it. Odin, gifted but very hot-blooded, posed some serious problems on account of his excitability. The effet d'ensemble has contributed to a great extent to his submission because it gave me an effective, non-violent means to 'bring him back to his senses' and 'on the aids', when his surroundings caused him to start to boil over. 'Merci, Monsieur Baucher.'

Final considerations

Regarding the 'well trained horse', if one wanted to summarise the goal as well as the means in a short formula, one could say:

The rider must have:
- Butter in his gloves
- Fire in his boots
- Balancing scales in his seat
- And a metronome in his head

To conclude this examination of the 'school of the aids', we must consider an equestrian concept that is difficult to grasp and often leads to misunderstandings: 'tone'.

This is one of those words which riding instructors and coaches repeat incessantly: 'The horse lacks swing – it is not in balance – it doesn't have enough tone ...!' If one doesn't know exactly what they are talking about, these words are cheap because even if they are not always quite right, they are also never totally wrong.

Under the pretext that the horse must be 'pushed' with the legs 'on to the hand', one can very easily confuse 'tone in the horse' with 'tension in the reins'. On this subject the image of a spring is rather appropriate:
- if a spring is too compressed, for too long, it loses its ability to extend, the origin of its strength;
- if stretched too far and too long, it quickly loses its flexibility, the essential quality that gives it its 'springiness'.

With a spring, strength and flexibility are inseparably connected in mutual dependence. If one wishes to use it optimally as a source of movement, one must stretch and release it, compress and extend it with regularity. Otherwise one damages it.

Just like a spring, the horse is only as good as the ease with which one can use him. In other words: depending on his strength and suppleness.

One must, therefore 'intimately connect impulsion to the flexibility of the joints' (Alexis L'Hotte).

Between 'leaning on the bit' on the one hand (sign of lacking balance and source of resistances) and constant use of the legs, on the other hand (sign of insufficient impulsion), one finds a 'tense' rider on a horse 'carried' by the aids, but in no way real tone. And this is true even if advantageous basic gaits flatter to deceive.

For the 'living spring' horse, an appropriate definition of tone must take into consideration both physical constitution and psychology. Hence, this equestrian concept suggests that 'tone' and 'attention' are synonymous.

Tone

Physically it is expressed by the supple, variable, lively stretch of the top line. It causes the mise en main and engagement of the hindquarters. In concrete terms, the 'toned' horse is always ready to push his poll over his mouth, to round and stretch his neck as well and always keen to flex the croup and bring his hocks under the mass.

Attention

Psychologically, the more the horse is concentrated on his rider and attentive to the aids, the easier he is to ride. Logically, the degree of attention that the horse pays to the aids can be measured by the degree of lightness (légèreté) that he exhibits.
- light to the legs: impulsion;
- light to the hand: relaxation and balance.

Tone and légèreté are not, therefore, incompatible. On the contrary, the lighter the horse is to the aids, the more freedom the rider has to generate tone.

Three of the biggest names from the long list of Masters of French equitation confirm this and define at the same time the 'well-trained horse':
- La Guérinière: 'keen in the haunches and gallant in the mouth'.
- Baucher: 'in front of the legs and behind the hand.' (Which here does not mean 'behind the bit', but rather 'on the aids'.)
- L'Hotte: 'The horse keeps himself behind the hand while growing taller at the same time as staying in front of the legs.'

Anyone seeking this useful 'tone' in a horse will find it, therefore, between lightness to the hand and lightness to the leg and one cannot have the one without the other.

Unfortunately this concept of légèreté which was seen again and again in the works of the most famous masters of the 'French tradition' has had no place in the FEI dressage regulations since 1958 (even though in the first issue of 1932, article 83 states: 'In all gaits a light mobility of the jaw, without any nervousness, is a proof of the horse's obedience and the harmonious distribution of his forces.') and is also no longer part of official riding education in France. One noteworthy book, which appeared in 1975, has the courage to defend it. It is entitled L'équitation de tradition française, but it comes from the hand of a Portuguese riding master, Diogo de Bragança.

From lack of understanding, if not out of ignorance or disdain, it is currently popular to regard a taste for légèreté as an 'outdated obsession', when in fact it is a constant search for effectiveness and efficiency of means.

Under the combined influences of the pressure of popular culture and the desire for rebellion – a luxury of spoilt children – we are destroying the very basis of our equestrian inheritance on which its wealth and originality are based. It would be naive to think that nebulous or formulaic 'educational reforms' can make up in the least for this abandoning of methodology and technical dumbing down.

Whether one likes it or not, egalitarianism and standardisation rarely lead to progress and creativity, but rather to an insidious cultural regression. In this case, and without wishing to cultivate a paradox, one can see that progress would be found in a return to 'our' (French) roots.

One cannot decently claim a cultural heritage and then not, at the same time, put it into practice. Some people will judge this a presumptive attitude but will have to admit that one is in rather good company there, since it is to Colonel P. Durand that we owe these lines, published in 1984:

The philosophy of academic equitation

'Since the 18th century and presumably even before that, the French manner consisted of putting the horse at "liberty on parole" (descente de main), after one had brought him into balance. It appears then that the French manner is a million miles away from any thoughts of primitive compulsion. It is a way of riding that is infinitely more elegant, aristocratic in the etymological sense but also more demanding: noblesse oblige. It requires much more care to look effortless than to just slave away.'

If horses were suddenly able to speak (and of course, for that to happen one would have to loosen their nosebands and yield with the hands ...), they would undoubtedly plead in favour of légèreté!

On the part of the rider, even more than a technical option, it is a fundamental question of culture and taste. It is légèreté, after all, that distinguishes ballet from gymnastics and Mozart from Wagner.

Style is everything, if one considers horse riding to be an expression of visual art, because it alone distinguishes the essentials.

'Style is a depth which reaches all the way to the surface.' *(Victor Hugo)*

'The mirror ought to reflect before revealing its image' (J. Cocteau)

Achilles' stallion

They say that humour is 'the elegance of despair'. Despite it being a distant memory, I still need a little humour today to describe what happened in 1987.

As it was, although Odin was integrated perfectly into the presentations of the Cadre Noir, the continuation of our association was by no means guaranteed. The problem was that the stallion was not owned by the state. He was, as one knows, a keen servant of it, but one could not with decency expect his owners to maintain him for ever, even for the glory of the School. M. and Mme. Huré informed me with all possible sensitivity that they had to put Odin up for sale. Not having the means to buy him myself, the École Nationale d'Équitation had to be informed that, if it wished to retain the pleasure of his company, it would have to buy him.

It should not have been a problem – because the National Stud financed the purchase of around 35 horses per year, and Odin, although unique for his kind, could still be had for a very reasonable price. Colonel Durand proposed buying him straight away.

But what seemed like a 'done deal' became an odyssey. The central management of the National Stud made it known that it grants money for the purchase of French horses, and not for the support of foreign breeds. I objected immediately that the horse was bred in France in a famous stud – that the School had often bought imported English Thoroughbreds – that in the middle of the construction of the European Community and a Common Agricultural Policy, such a position smacked somewhat of a protectionist rearguard action.

Colonel Durand also pleaded our cause with just as much conviction, though without a doubt more diplomatically, but nothing helped. I was about to lose my best horse and the Cadre Noir an original and successful presentation, and all because of some red tape!

Fortunately, he did not give up and devised, with support from J-F. Charry who was at that time president of the French Equestrian Federation, the only possible alternative. Odin's contribution to the School's income was booked in the budget under an account entitled 'presentations'. The account showed big profits, so logically one could consider purchasing the horse from these funds.

To be sure that this transaction would be acceptable under the rules of management of public funds, the Colonel requested financial approval from the ministry of youth and sport. What the 'horse people' had refused, the 'administrative people' permitted. We had the green light! Thus, at the end of 1987, Odin became the property of the École Nationale d'Équitation.

Need I say how relieved I was, and how grateful I remain to Colonel Durand? He was willing to fight where others hid behind caution and timidity.

The recollection of this skirmish gives me the chance to pay tribute to him, and never fails to remind me of the words of Saint-Exupéry: 'They did not know it was impossible, so they did it.'

But the story would not be complete without its epilogue. Some years later, on the occasion of a visit to the seat of the National Stud in Paris, I proposed a collaboration between that office and the École Nationale d'Équitation in order to make an assessment of French stallions on the basis of their aptitude for dressage by means of the performances of the Cadre Noir. My suggestion was well received even if, for reasons that would take too long to explain, it was never realised.

The representative of the National Stud who received me, and whose name I have tactfully forgotten, literally said to me: 'This is an interesting idea – because for us your grey there is not a horse, but a theatrical accessory!' Interminable resentment. Operatic dancers will appreciate the comparison. I would have liked to have reminded this illustrious civil servant what one ordinarily calls someone who denigrates a particular race, but I bit my tongue and thought that one can sometimes wonder whether it is really man who is 'the horse's most noble conquest'.

That said, I made an effort to put the idea into practice. My argument was that Odin was getting older and one had to think of retiring him and of replacing him one day. And so, the new manager, M. Lhemanne, agreed to the School acquiring an understudy to the 'theatrical accessory'. After the usual procedure we acquired a second four-year-old, grey, Lusitano stallion in 1992. He was bred by J. Peigné, and called, somewhat ironically, Verdi. Our destiny was undoubtedly on the stage!

In the end, as everyone knows, 'Nothing is lost, nothing is created, everything changes', and it is sometimes quite pleasant to see how history straightens things out.

In 1992, at the Olympic games in Barcelona, Orphée, a pure-bred Lusitano stallion, half-brother of Odin and from the same stud, was a member of the French dressage team. The stallion, trained by Michel Henriquet and ridden by Catherine Durand, came twenty-fifth out of fifty participants. Let's just say that he was the best placed of all the horses 'born in France'. Birth rights have their advantages! In the next year the same pair won the French Kür to music championships. Another pleasant 'coup de théâtre'!

At the Olympic games in Atlanta, all four members of the French dressage team rode German horses. I have nothing against that, but it is nevertheless something that should make the zealous defenders of 'French breeding' think and encourage them not to miss the mark for lack of making good choices.

Because I was tired of hearing the perfidious and pathetic little criticisms muttered over and over again: 'these are circus horses – trained monkeys – cuddly toys on wheels – competition riding is much more difficult than presentations', I decided to take all the purveyors of convenient opinions and quick prejudices at their word.

Pesade in the park of Karlsruhe castle

Verdi in piaffe

... in passage

... and in extended trot

Achilles' stallion

And so in 1994 Odin took part for the first time in a dressage test. For seven years he had risen to the challenge of an extensive show programme, thanks to which I knew perfectly well there was no need to participate in the competition circuit.

His first competition was the National de Saumur in May. He achieved fourth place in the Grand Prix freestyle to music. In his second competition, the National de Paris in June, he won the Grand Prix freestyle to music. The height of irony was that on this occasion I won a week's holiday for two – in Andalusia! I had never set foot there before, and naturally I took the opportunity to extend my vacation with a week at the Royal Andalusian School in Jerez, where I was wonderfully welcomed by Don Alvaro Domecq.

The following year, Odin was entered in the international dressage competition at Saumur which took place two weeks before an important trip to Paris-Bercy. Unfortunately, in the days before the competition the vet diagnosed the beginnings of bronchitis. His verdict was: in principle, no absolute ban on competing, but increased risk of deterioration, and with it the danger that he might not be able to participate at Bercy. I had to decide: either take part in the international dressage competition, or prioritise the three evenings in Paris (with Odin as a soloist twice per evening in front of eight to ten thousand spectators, accompanied by a symphony orchestra).

I withdrew him from the competition and chose the stage at Bercy, surrounded by an audience, instead of a letter-framed rectangle. A wise decision, because after all, 'the spirit is more important than the letter'.

The Paris audience, the 'theatrical accessory' and I all felt so, anyway.

Lateral suppling exercises

Since correct balance and the optimum use of the horse assume relaxation, suppleness and straightness, one must guide the horse through a gymnastic development designed to increase flexibility, to harmonise his forces and finally to redress his natural asymmetry as much as possible.

A pianist or dancer, irrespective of whether they are right- or left-handed, must work on becoming virtually ambidextrous – the same applies to the horse.

The term 'lateral work' covers all those exercises that relate lateral bending of the spine with movement on two tracks.

For example, one can easily imagine that, for a horse that is naturally hollow on the left, work in a right bend is vital. One should not conclude that one has to keep the horse constantly on a circle on the right rein, however, because this right bend, if maintained for too long, will automatically lead to resistances due to tensions, cramps and muscular aches. The physiology of muscles teaches us that a very pronounced but brief bending is substantially easier and more beneficial than one that is imposed for longer, even if it is less pronounced.

Never forget that 'gymnastic' training consists of repeating movements and extending their range rather than holding certain postures for a long time – however 'correct' they may be. This means that in order to achieve a yielding, it is preferable to make frequent changes of bend while maintaining the same circle. Wearisome training based on 'doing the miles' should be rejected, then, in favour of a gymnastic education through repetition. Knowing that a treatment can only be as good as the accuracy of the diagnosis, one should begin by accurately describing the problem.

In the case which interests us, a certain 'Odin', we find the following basic facts:

Naturally bent to the left
· Head carried to the left.
· Falls out through the right shoulder.
· Hindquarters displaced to the left. Left hind leg engages more than it pushes, the right hind leg pushes more than it engages.
· The right diagonal leg pair is advanced.

A rational gymnastic programme must consist of choosing and carefully adapting exercises that cause exactly the opposite of all these asymmetries, in order to gradually reduce them.

At first glance the programme must include:
- More frequent and pronounced bending to the right. Limited frequency and degree of left bending.
- Frequent transfers of weight onto the left shoulder. Reduce the time spent with weight on the right shoulder.
- Develop the push of the left hind leg and the engagement of the right hind leg.
- Develop the range of movement of the left diagonal leg pair (example: rising with the left diagonal in the trot).

The guiding principle must remain: 'proceed from the simple to the complex'. The exercises are developed progressively, beginning with those where the natural balance is sufficient and progressing to those that require more and more collection. One begins them at the walk, then proceeding to the trot and finally, the canter.

That said, the equestrian tact and intelligence of the rider permit him to invent all kinds of combinations of figures, provided that they serve to make the horse more symmetrical and develop mobility in all directions.

There is an infinite range of possibilities, and the aim here cannot be to create an exhaustive list. I will, therefore, only stress the important points that one should pay attention to for each of the major exercises, so that one can play them off against each other and bring the horse as quickly as possible to perform them symmetrically.

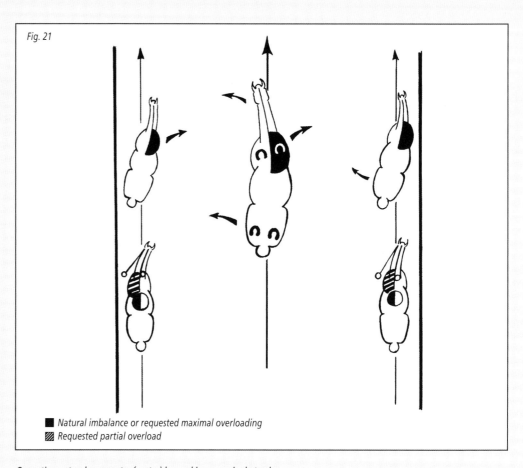

Fig. 21

■ *Natural imbalance or requested maximal overloading*
▨ *Requested partial overload*

Correcting natural asymmetry (centre) by working on a single track

Work on a single track

Since the horse is naturally bent to the left and crooked to the left, the rider must strive to straighten the posture from beginning of the work, by straightening the neck and placing the shoulders in front of the hindquarters.

Straight lines

On the left rein

The horse stays on the track quite happily but with his outside shoulder sticking out towards the walls and his head and hindquarters towards the inside.

Straighten the neck, or even bend it slightly outwards to send the shoulders back to the inside by a right indirect rein effect, perhaps supported by a left opening rein to lead the shoulders inwards. If necessary, the rider can also use his seat by sitting with his weight to the left.

On the right rein

The horse tends to come in from the track. If not, he at least goes with his head and hindquarters towards the outside.

Bend the neck clearly to the inside and with the help of the right indirect rein (perhaps supported by the left opening rein), send the shoulders back to the outside. This is what Steinbrecht calls the 'bent-straight' position (neck bent, horse on a single track). The seat helps with weight transfer to the outside.

These straightening exercises must be repeated as often as necessary, but must not be maintained too long. Change the rein very frequently. At this stage it would be wrong to think the legs could contribute something to the straightening of the horse. They must simply maintain the regularity of movement.

Curved lines

Of course, the techniques used on straight lines can also be employed on curves, but with more precision and variety.

Lateral suppling exercises

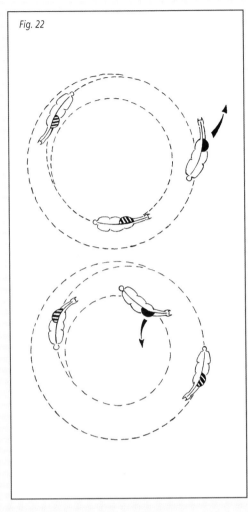

Fig. 22

Correcting natural asymmetry on a circle

Work on the circle

On the left rein

This is the easier side. However, the horse will tend to increase the diameter of the circle by bending his neck inwards and falling out through his outside shoulder.
Therefore:
• put the horse into a counter-bend;
• shift weight onto the inside shoulder, using the right indirect rein, in order to reduce the size of the circle;
• make use of the seat by sitting to the inside;
• as a preventative measure, use a slight counter-bend as preparation for a circle to the left.

On the right rein

This is the less easy side. The horse tends to tighten the circle by falling onto his inside shoulder and carrying his neck to the outside. He turns by a 'loss of balance':
• use a distinct bend to the right;
• use the right indirect rein to shift weight to the outside shoulder and enlarge the circle;
• encourage the transfer of weight by sitting to the outside;
• as a preventative measure, prepare for a circle to the right with the 'bent-straight' position.

Impact and applications

Since passing through a corner is the same as riding a quarter of a circle, it should be prepared for and executed just like beginning a circle.

Decreasing and increasing the size of the circle are the bases of all the lateral suppling exercises. Practised at the walk and trot, they enable the rider to tackle a critical task: straightening the canter.

We know that with the horse who is naturally bent to the left:

... the left-lead canter increases the displacement of the haunches: reducing the size of the circle by the judicious use of counter-bending can be used here to bring the left shoulder in front of the left hip;

... the right-lead canter contributes to overall straightening: nevertheless, if the horse is allowed to turn by 'losing his balance' it will destroy this positive effect and sometimes lead to a change of lead in the hindquarters and cross-cantering. Increasing the size of the circle with the help of a clear right bend favours the alignment of the left lateral leg pair and with it the restoration of the balance.

The figure of eight

The clever combination of circles to the left and the right leads to many possibilities:
• variations in diameter (big circles on one rein, smaller on the other);
• variations in the sequence (two circles on one rein, one on the other);

Correcting natural asymmetry on a figure eight

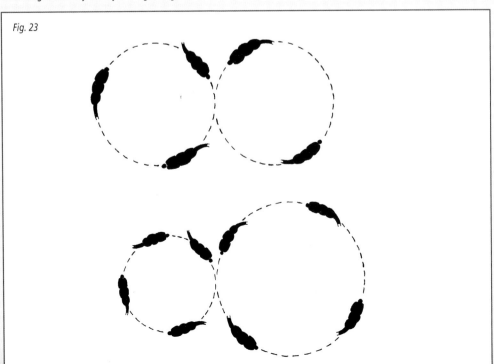

Fig. 23

- variations in the bend (true bend on one rein, counter-bend on the other).

The combinations can be infinitely varied with the aim of achieving the perfect figure of eight. Examples: perform a figure of eight and:
- change from the circle on the left rein left to the circle on the right rein right by anticipating the change of bend;
- change from the circle on the right rein left to the circle on the left rein right by delaying the change of bend.

Serpentines

All these possibilities can also be used, of course, on serpentines, until a harmonious, symmetrical pattern can be achieved.
Example:
- on the right rein: big curves with a clear bend;
- on the left rein: tighter curves in counter-bend, etc.

The horse that is able to perform tighter and tighter turns in either bend gains in suppleness and becomes agile.

Work on two tracks

After he has begun straightening the horse by the forehand, that is to say, putting the shoulders in front of the haunches, the rider gradually brings the hindquarters under control through work on two tracks: lateral movements in all directions and in all possible postures. The activation and control of the hindquarters are fundamentally important for the schooling of collection.

However fundamental it may be, work on two tracks also has its limits and some conditions that must be fulfilled. Every lateral movement is performed at the expense of forward thrust (at the risk of stating the blindingly obvious). Thus, one should not exaggerate them because that would run the risk of developing suppleness at the expense of impulsion. Hence, one gets the best out of lateral work if one changes frequently between work on one and two tracks and is careful not to allow the activity to decrease.

A characteristic of work on two tracks is the crossing of the limbs. As far as the hindquarters are concerned, this means the strides lose in engagement what they gain in crossing. Now, it is this active engagement of the hind legs that prepares the horse for collection by bringing him into better balance while preserving impulsion. Hence, one should limit the angle of displacement in lateral exercises, so that they improve engagement under the mass instead of encouraging more cross-over. These conditions are fulfilled if the horse moves approximately on 'three tracks'. Visually, useful crossing is evident from the length of the strides and not from an excessive angle of displacement.

So, we can see that, in this case, 'more' is not necessarily 'better'.

Every exercise on two tracks must be evaluated according to:
- the changes of balance that it requires;
- the horse's asymmetries and the tendencies for which one must compensate;
- purpose and value within the gymnastic development plan;
- on each rein: the horse's natural tendencies and the compensations necessary;
- respective impact and areas of special consideration.

From this information, the rider can decide what aids he must apply to achieve, in the end, symmetry of execution and, therefore, straightness.

Yielding of the haunches

Begun on the circle by gradually rotating the hindquarters around the forehand, far from disturbing the horse's natural balance, this exercise even confirms it. As a starting point of lateral work, yielding the haunches enables the rider to educate the horse to the single leg. It is taught at first at the walk, in-hand if necessary.

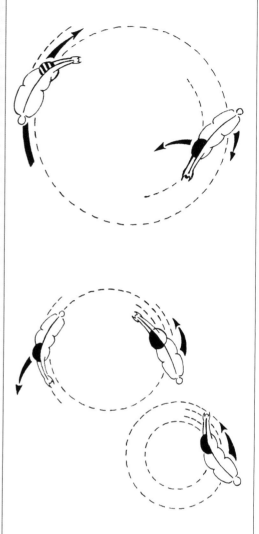

Fig. 24

Yielding of the haunches in shoulder-in and renvers position

Shoulder-in position

An extremely important position since, if performed with a constant angle, the shoulder-in is the lateral exercise which most favours the engagement and limits the degree of crossover.

On the right rein

The horse tends to straighten his neck and reduce the size of the circle while falling onto the inside shoulder and skidding the haunches outwards as it hesitates.
Therefore:
• Ask for the yielding of the haunches on a bigger circle and ride well forwards.
• Use a pronounced bend to send the horse back onto the outside shoulder.
• Use the right leg acting at the girth to ask for a limited yielding of the quarters.

On the left rein

The horse tends to 'break' his neck, fall out through his outside shoulder, and struggles to move the haunches to the outside.
Therefore:
• Work on a small circle executed at the 'counted walk'.
• Use the outside indirect rein to limit the bend and press the horse inwards, so that his left shoulder becomes loaded and stabilises.
• Demand a clear yielding of the left hind leg, by associating the left leg aids with support from the whip on the inside thigh.

Renvers (haunches out)

Yielding of the haunches while bent to the outside is of particular interest on the left rein. In effect, it is the exact opposite of the horse's natural tendency and therefore constitutes an excellent corrective. On the right rein, however, this position reinforces the horse's natural asymmetry and is, therefore, the one possibility without real benefit in this case.

On the left rein

Work on a small circle at the counted walk. Load the left shoulder as much as possible through the use of a pronounced right bend, and shift the shoulders to the inside using the right indirect rein. Reinforce the yielding of the haunches and crossing of the hind legs using the left leg in isolation, acting behind the girth. The exercise must develop the incurvation of the horse towards the right, with the load remaining clearly on the left shoulder.

Impact and applications

The rotation around the shoulders causes a transfer of weight onto the forehand. The smaller the circle and the more one approaches the reverse pirouette, the more weight is transferred to the shoulders which become 'fixed'. From this, one can derive two areas of application:
• In combination with the bend to the right, the exercise leads to an inevitable stretching of the neck. Even with the most recalcitrant horses this way of working succeeds in achieving the extension of the neck because it arises from a gymnastic practice and not from direct pressure. Yielding the haunches saves one from having to force a posture by the use of auxiliary reins.
• Yielding the haunches is the 'anti-rearing' solution par excellence. In effect, by removing the prop necessary for this rebellion and obliging the horse to put his weight on the forehand with his neck extended, the rider turns the situation around in his favour. This is a little like the actions and understanding of a judo expert – which will work better in this situation than approaching the horse with the mind of a wrestler.

A horse that evades, by rushing at the walk or the trot, can be quickly led back to a regular tempo by yielding the haunches. Because the hindquarters must step around the slowed down forehand, the strength of the push is diverted and split. It is an application of the famous 'divide and conquer' principle – but in this case for a noble purpose.

Horses that tend to 'amble' (lateralise the walk by hurrying with the forelegs and trailing the hind legs with a contracted back), find their way back to a regular four-beat walk thanks to the shoulder-in on the circle. With the forehand 'fixed', the horse takes short, slow steps. At the same time it must extend the strides of the hind legs as they go around the larger circle. The resulting lengthening of the neck stretches and loosens the back. It provides the perfect antidote to 'ambling'.

Shoulder-in position on the straight line

If the horse understands the role of the sideways driving leg acting at the girth, which stimulates the hindquarters and contributes to the overall bend, one can tackle the shoulder-in on a straight line. This exercise helps to develop the engagement of the inside hind leg and the overall bend, to put the horse on the inside haunch and relieve the shoulders.

Shoulder-in

On the right rein

The horse tends to straighten the bend and falls onto his inside shoulder, and the hindquarters evade by a sideways displacement of the outside hind leg. The right hind leg crosses more than it engages.
Therefore:
• A clear right bend and the right indirect rein bring the horse more onto the outside shoulder.
• Limit the angle of displacement to approximately three tracks. This ensures the best engagement of the right hind leg under the mass in the direction of the left foreleg.

On the left rein

The horse tends to overbend his neck with his shoulders falling to the outside and his hindquarters falling to the inside of the arena.
Therefore:
• Limit the bend and increase the loading on the left shoulder with the help of the right indirect rein which leads the shoulders clearly away from the wall.

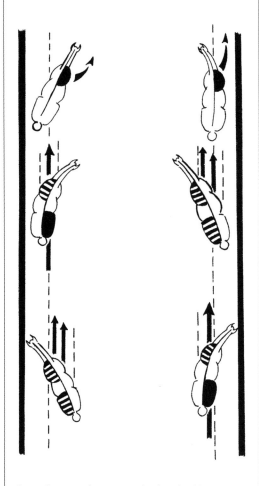

Correcting natural asymmetry (top) in shoulder-in (middle) and counter shoulder-in (bottom) on a straight line

Fig. 25

• Insist on obedience to the left leg acting in isolation at the girth, and reinforce the yielding of the inside haunch until the movement is clearly performed on four tracks. This reinforced crossing teaches the horse to yield correctly with the left hind leg and to begin to straighten himself.

Counter shoulder-in

For the horse the task is, in principle, the same. For the rider, the two situations differ. In the shoulder-in, the horse's hindquarters are channelled by the walls, in the counter shoulder-in the forehand is guided by the walls. So, the rider can alternate the two positions according to his needs, knowing that the counter shoulder-in left makes mobilisation of the haunches easier, while counter shoulder-in right facilitates movement of the shoulders.

Effects and applications

Shoulder-in straightens and bends, develops suppleness and improves the horse's balance in forward movement. It allows a progressive development of collection in all three gaits. It has the significant advantage of splitting up the difficulties since, in the shoulder-in, the horse is collected, so to speak, one half at a time.

Shoulder-in is the 'trot position' (Gustav Steinbrecht). In effect, if a horse breaks from the trot to the canter and remains there in spite of the rider's efforts (for example, on the left rein), one must only put it in to (left) shoulder-in position in order to bring it back to the trot immediately and without a struggle. This position, which puts the right lateral leg pair ahead of the left, makes the horse cross the legs to the right and interferes significantly with the mechanics of the left-lead canter – and the horse chooses to change back to the trot. A solution based on the absolute fundamentals.

A shallow shoulder-in (with a small angle of displacement, known by some as 'shoulder-fore') contributes efficiently to the straightening and collection of the canter. In the case of the horse that is naturally bent to the left, left shoulder-in favours above all the straightening of the left-lead canter, while right shoulder-in promotes the collection of right-lead canter.

Haunches-in on the circle

By practising the shoulder-in, the horse has learned to bend around the inside leg at the girth and made his first attempts at collection.

To progress further, one must now confirm the bend, with the outside leg taking over the control of the hindquarters, and increase collection by rotating the forehand around the hindquarters.

Travers

The exercise consists of bringing the haunches to the inside of the circle while keeping the horse bent in the direction of movement (half-pass position).

On the left rein

The horse is naturally at ease in this position since it corresponds to his natural bend. However, he will tend to overbend the neck, increase the size of the circle and bring the haunches too much to the inside.
Therefore:
• Work on a circle of limited diameter and keep the horse going forwards.
• Limit the bend and push the horse more onto the inside shoulder with the right indirect rein.
• Limit the angle of displacment (approximately three tracks), using only a little outside leg acting behind the girth and use the left leg at the girth to encourage forward movement.
Thus, the horse's forehand steps actively around the left haunch, which becomes increasingly 'fixed' and loaded instead of giving way.

On the right rein

The horse finds this position difficult at first, because it runs counter to his natural bend. He tries to bring his shoulders back in front of his hindquarters while reducing the size of the circle and straightening the bend of his neck.

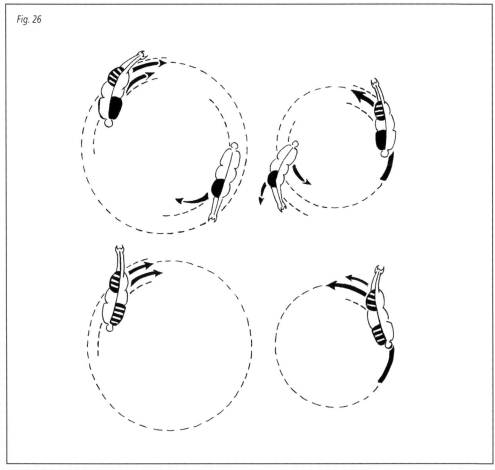

Fig. 26

Correcting natural asymmetry in travers on the circle

Therefore:
• Work on a large circle with a clear right bend.
• Keep the shoulders on the circle of reference by the right indirect rein.
• Insist on a clear yielding of the hindquarters to the action of the left leg behind the girth, supported if necessary by the whip on the horse's left thigh. Work on four tracks, so that the horse shifts the croup clearly inwards and carries the load on the inside haunch instead of pushing off with the outside hind leg.

Impact and application
Travers is the 'canter position' (Gustav Steinbrecht). Indeed, travers favours the canter, just as the canter makes travers easier.

For example: for a horse that is naturally strongly bent to the left and struggles particularly with the right-lead canter, a large circle in travers brings the right lateral leg pair in front of the left one. From this posture the horse can only depart into the right-lead canter and not counter-canter or go disunited. Encouraging the canter, promoting bend and placing the horse on the hindquarters, this position is especially useful for developing the walk-canter transition and improving collection.

Counter shoulder-in position
This is a variation where the horse brings his hindquarters to the inside of the circle but remains bent in the opposite direction to the movement. Compared to the travers, this position makes it easier to bring the hindquarters in because the hind leg on the inside of the circle takes up less load and the outside hind crosses over less. It does, however, require greater crossing of the forelegs.
Thus: by means of the usual precautions:
• keep the circle on the right rein larger than on the left rein;
• above all, this position is of interest for developing the hindquarters on the right rein and the mobility of the shoulders on the left rein.

Half-pass

For the horse, the half-pass consists of following a straight line on two tracks while bent in the direction of movement and while maintaining consistent bend, angle of displacement and cadence. Cadence is important because the half-pass does not contribute to collection but rather requires it to express itself optimally. The half-pass is really the most difficult exercise on two tracks. It shows exactly what degree of suppleness and collection the horse has reached. Because it is the 'end result' as well as the 'milestone' of work on two tracks, the half-pass is one of the airs demonstrated in presentations.

On the left rein
For our example horse this is actually the easier side. But he will tend to overbend his neck and keep his weight on the outside shoulder, while positioning himself at an extreme angle due to excessive movement of the hindquarters. The old masters said that a horse whose hindquarters go ahead of his shoulders like this becomes 'wedged together'.
Therefore:
• Prepare for half-pass to the left with the shoulder-in, so that the forehand leads.
• Limit the bend and bring the horse more on the internal shoulder by the right indirect rein.
• Limit the use of the right leg behind the girth and use the left leg at the girth more clearly to limit the sideways movement and encourage movement to the front.
• Limit the movement to three tracks

Half-pass to the right in trot on long reins

On the right rein

This is the more difficult side, since it opposes the horse's natural disposition. The horse will tend to wander off the intended line of travel, by straightening the bend of the neck, falling on the right shoulder and struggling against the movement of the hindquarters towards the right. The old masters said that a horse that tried to abandon the half-pass position by bringing the shoulders back in front of the haunches like this 'unwinds'.

Therefore:

• Prepare for the half-pass right with the 'bent-straight' position to guarantee the bend and at the same time bring the horse more onto his outside shoulder.

• Insist as a priority on obedience to the left leg acting behind the girth – even if the horse then begins to execute the half-pass with the hindquarters leading ('wedging' as an interim correction). Increase the angle to four tracks.

Maintain a clear right bend and limit the movement of the shoulders to the right by repeated interventions with the right indirect rein.

Head to the wall and tail to the wall

These are variations of the half-pass which can help with learning. In these positions the rider can use the walls to judge the angle of the horse more easily and to channel the forehand or hindquarters. That said, the same rules apply to their execution.

On the left rein, the rider must:

• limit the bend in 'head to the wall' and keep the displacement to three tracks;

• increase the bend in 'tail to the wall' and keep the forehand well away from the wall while moving on four tracks.

On the right rein, the rider must:

• increase the bend in the 'head to the wall', keeping the forehand towards the walls and shift the hindquarters out to execute the movement on four tracks;

• limit the degree of bend in the 'tail to the wall' and keep the angle to three tracks.

Observations

In teaching the half-pass, one will find the following most useful:
- head to the wall on the right rein;
- tail to the wall on the left rein.

Half-pass to the right in trot under saddle

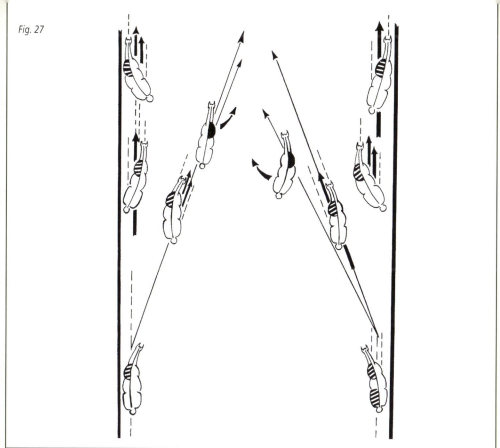

Correcting natural asymmetry in travers and half-pass

Since travers is, as we know, the 'canter position', a horse which finds the half-pass difficult will profit very much from practising it at the canter, with the aim of improving its execution at the trot.

Half-pass to the left profits from preparation in the shoulder-in, while the half-pass to the right is better initiated by the 'bent-straight' position or by a circle to the left in counter-bend.

The basic half-pass is executed more or less on three tracks. In order to preserve good balance, the angle can only be increased according to the degree of collection achieved.

In contrast, exaggerating the angle to improve the half-pass would be a mistake. Once again, 'more' is not necessarily 'better'. Indeed, either the horse has to 'crawl' through the half-pass, that is, without a suspension phase, or it performs the 'passage-trot' with a hollow back. The latter, while impressing the layman, indicates a defect in the collected trot as well as a falsification of the passage. These would represent a serious compromise of the overall training.

In conclusion

If one considers the education of the horse as a 'schooling of the aids' with attention to légèreté and with the aim of gymnastic correction of the natural asymmetry, one discovers that the famous polemics centred around the precedence of the 'lateral' or 'diagonal' aids become uninteresting, even pointless.

In academic equitation, the pursuit of straightness is at the same time the inevitable means and the end goal of – unattainable – perfection. D'Auvergne expressed it perfectly:

'The horseman with all the perfection of his art spends his life correcting this imperfection.'

From this, one sees that, at every step of the education, the trainer must organise the work so that he corrects the horse's asymmetries a little more each day because with every new exercise he will find the source of contractions to be resolved and difficulties to be overcome.

Galas and guest performances of the Cadre Noir

Between May 1986 and July 1998, Odin took part in all the Cadre Noir's public performances. Besides the shows which take place every two weeks from the beginning of April till the end of September in the National Riding School, where he was often presented in long reins, he had pride of place in all gala performances in Saumur, elsewhere in France and abroad.

Every year there are, on average, four Galas in Saumur itself, as well as two to three guest performances in France and abroad, each one comprising three presentations. During the course of each presentation Odin was seen in the historical sketch or in long reins – and frequently in both. This means that he was often flying solo for a good fifth of the show, though now and then with support from Verdi in later years.

Verdi in the arena at Nîmes

The honour of being introduced to the Queen of Spain

The most important guest performances in France were: Amiens, Cannes, Marcq-en-Baroeul, Lyons, Lille, Cherburg, Nîmes, twice at Versailles, twice in Paris-Bercy – or actually three times for Odin, who was the first to appear there on the occasion of the show jumping World Cup Finals in 1987.

Of all these guest performances in France, Versailles, Nîmes and Paris remain especially clear in my memory.

Versailles, because it was Odin's first guest appearance, in front of fantastic scenery, at the magical home of the equitation of one's dreams.

Nîmes also made an impression on me, because of the beauty of the Roman arena in which the presentations took place, the especially warm atmosphere of the feria – but also because it was here that Verdi supported Odin for the first time – successfully, too.

Paris-Bercy is a gigantic, very imposing sports palace. The event in 1995 impressed me the most. As was so often the case, Odin had two appearances per evening, but this time he performed a unique duet in long reins with the American singer Julia Migenes.

The latter, known among other things for her interpretation of Carmen in Francesco Rossi's film, reprised this role for Bercy, singing the most famous arias from Georges Bizet's masterpiece in the arena. With barely any experience of horses, Julia Migenes found Odin daunting and was seriously afraid to come near him. Because we had only two rehearsals, she came every evening to the stable and practised her scales in front of Odin's box while giving him tidbits to calm him. She won his trust, he profited from it. I, on the other hand, teased her with accusations of bribing a civil servant.

Julia Migenes and Odin head to head in Paris-Bercy

Galas and guest performances of the Cadre Noir

Seville. Pesade in front of the royal box

In spite of all these precautions, Odin was the cause of an incident during the dress rehearsal. I was supposed to present him while accompanying Julia's movements in the arena, which did not simplify our task. On this evening, she was wearing a beautiful black satin gown that shimmered every time she moved under the floodlights. Odin, worried by this, stubbornly refused to go anywhere near her. Time was pressing, and the presentation threatened to become a disaster. Was it that he wanted to be the only one to shine? Nonetheless, Julia had to quickly exchange her satin gown for something much plainer made out of matt black material. Odin appeared satisfied with this concession from the Diva and kept his own white dinner jacket!

The most important foreign guest performances were: Milan, Wembley, Mondorf, Essen, Mannheim, Berlin, Munich, Münster, Karlsruhe, three times in Brussels and Seville. Each had its own charm, but three of them stick especially in my memory:

Karlsruhe, because the presentations took place in front of the illuminated Baroque facade of the castle: a background of rare beauty.

Berlin, because it was there that Odin was presented for the first time outside of Saumur on long reins. He was, in fact, the first horse of the Cadre Noir to present the High School airs in this manner: work on two tracks, pirouettes, passage, piaffe, pesade, exiting the arena in Spanish walk.

Seville, because there Odin was close to the land of his forefathers and because Queen Sofia, to whom we had the honour of being introduced, attended the presentations. Although very much loved by the Spanish, Queen Sofia is of Greek descent, a heritage that had left her with a deep aversion to bullfighting. She had, therefore, always refused to preside over a corrida. Finally, thanks to our performances, the members of the maestranza of Seville finally had the satisfaction of seeing their Queen honour the rostrums of the arena with her presence.

There are some miracles only horses can perform.

Exercises for longitudinal flexibility

Lateral suppling exercises develop above all the suppleness in the horizontal plane. Through riding circles and lateral exercises the rider gains control of the direction of movement, initiates the first changes of balance and begins to straighten the horse.

The longitudinal suppling exercises cultivate primarily the horse's flexibility in the vertical plane. Exercising the whole range of transitions enables the rider to bring the speed under control and leads to the complete mastery of balance that determines the manoeuvrability of the horse.

Transitions

Transitions are the exercises that consist of changing from one gait to another or varying the speed within a gait. They are tests of the horse's légèreté and of his ability to change his balance.

Transitions within a gait

Here we are concerned with 'lengthening and shortening of the gaits'. The two cannot be separated, because lengthening the gait or extending the strides is only conceivable with the complementary ability to be able to shorten them again.

If one wants to judge the education of a horse, the extension of the strides is much less interesting than the way in which it he does it and comes back again. In fact, spectacular lengthening demonstrates above all the horse's innate abilities, while that which precedes and follows reveals more about the level of education achieved.

In upwards transitions, the horse expresses his degree of tone: always ready to go in front of the leg (impulsion) and always ready to extend the neck over the mouth in search of the contact with the rider's hand. In downwards transitions the horse shows his degree of balance: allowing the rider to 'retake' him with fluidity and relaxation (mise en main) and without even thinking of losing activity (collection).

One can see that a horse who is able to perform repeated and close-interval transitions promptly and fluidly in just a few strides shows a substantially higher level of balance and légèreté than another that can cover 50 metres in spectacular strides but is laborious in the upwards transition and, above all, heavy in the downwards transition.

From this we can deduce that prolonged lengthening is of dubious interest, since it is of little use during training except for its value in a dressage test. Nevertheless, the sport of dressage pushes riders into premature exploitation of the basic gaits that is to the detriment of the fundamentals and the long-term, causing the horses to be braced, overloaded and thrown on the forehand.

Lengthening over extended distances ought to be regarded therefore as an end product, an 'air', for horses that have reached a high level of education.

Transitions between gaits

Just as for transitions within a gait, downwards transitions between the gaits turn out to be more difficult and more indicative than upwards ones. Let's take the extreme example of the canter.

Upwards transition

Rudimentary transitions are obtained from the trot. Transitions from the walk and then from the halt can be performed relatively easily if the horse is only light enough to the leg and stretches willingly. This corresponds to quite a low level of education. Things are quite different in the opposite direction, however.

Downwards transition

From the canter to the trot – an easy transition that can be achieved just by slowing the canter. Lazy horses even tend to do this themselves.

From the canter to the walk – performed correctly, this transition requires that the horse can canter energetically at the speed of the walk. This implies a certain degree of collection.

From the canter to the halt – a difficult transition whose fluid execution assumes that the horse can canter practically in place. This corresponds to a high degree of collection – about as much as is required for pirouettes.

Nevertheless, numerous tests include transitions from canter to the halt on the programme, for horses and sometimes also riders who are still far from approaching even the beginnings of a pirouette.

Underestimating the difficulty like this is a mistake on the part of the person responsible for designing the test and reveals insufficient mastery of the subject; it encourages the competition participants to force the transition with a hard hand – with all its negative consequences for the education of the horse as well as the rider.

Progression of the work

As a cornerstone of the horse's gymnastic training, transitions must be carefully and rationally factored into the plan over the entire course of education. Since lateral flexibility also develops flexibility in the longitudinal plane, one can make use of the advantages of one to divide and resolve the difficulties of the other.

Simple transitions

Here we are concerned with the first transitions in the basic phase of education. The rider is careful not to disturb the horse's natural balance and to keep it round and relaxed.

Precautions

- Before attempting any transition in a straight line, the horse must be able to perform it perfectly on a circle on both reins.
- With the help of the further compensatory gymnastics discussed above, the rider on the circle can take advantage of relative straightness and can make use of the bend.
- If the horse remains bent through his body, it is practically impossible for him to hollow his top line in the course of the transition. Thus he learns to remain correctly mise en main and to lift his back in the transition.

Execution

Apart from the aids required for steering the horse, the rider must follow the principle 'hand without legs, legs without hand'.

Upwards transitions

Halt → walk → trot → canter ...
then: halt → trot and walk → canter.
Lighten the load on the back using all possible means, in particular by rising to the trot and by using neck extension. Avoid aids that surprise the horse, because they cause bracing and disturb the movement. Hence, prepare for every transition and draw the horse's attention by requesting the yielding of the jaw and checking the neck extension.

Downwards transitions

Canter → trot → walk → halt.
Before every transition, ask for the yielding of the jaw and then shorten the gait little by little by stretching up and playing with the fingers on the reins. The legs stay in contact but remain passive. By slowing down, the horse falls back into the lower gait. If the horse does not respond: do not make the aids stronger because that would only make the horse hollow, but enforce the transition by reducing the size of the circle and, if necessary, by displacing the hindquarters. Use authority without aggression. If the horse anticipates the transition, immediately send it energetically forward again in the higher gait. If he falls lazily into the lower gait, systematically associate the transition with energetic lengthening.

Advantages and uses

The qualities of one gait can be used to improve another.

The horse with a lazy walk

By making very frequent transitions between some strides at the walk and a brisk trot, one can achieve significant results. Since the horse knows that he may be asked to take an energetic trot at any moment, he will be inclined to maintain a lively, alert walk – which serves him at the same time as a reward, since it saves the rider from having to constantly 'push' the walk, and all the disadvantages that entails.

The horse that 'runs' with flat strides at the trot

The gait lacks suspension, the movement is expressionless and the horse tends to rush. Knowing that the canter is the gait in which the horse's spine oscillates the most in the vertical plane, frequent transitions between a few strides of trot and some brief sequences of forwards canter will increase the brilliance of the trot. The canter thus inspires the horse to use his back better at the trot.

In conclusion

Every gait creates an 'echo', a resonance, in the one that follows. One should make use of this phenomenon. By doing so, the rider can improve the transitions and the quality of the gaits at the same time. As the training progresses, the transitions can be condensed, little by little. For example: reducing the number of trot strides between canter and walk or the number of strides of walk between trot and halt.

More advanced transitions

Once the simple transition is developed far enough that the horse remains round, it then becomes a matter of having the haunches cooperate by engaging further under the mass. With the knowledge that training progresses much more efficiently the more one works progressively, one should make things easier for the pupil by dividing up the difficulties.

Now the rider makes use of the exercises that develop lateral suppleness to gradually promote the flexion and active engagement of the hind legs under the mass – that is to say, one after the other, and with a very gradual addition of the extra load. Thus, thanks to the careful choice of lateral exercises, the horse will be learning how to shorten a gait or perform a downwards transition by the engagement of a single hind leg.

Transitions in shoulder-in on a straight line

It should come as no surprise that the shoulder-in – the 'trot position' that promotes the diagonalisation of the gait – is the ideal exercise for the step-by-step development of collection. Transitions performed in the shoulder-in (on three tracks):
• keep the horse incurved, round and mise en main;
• preserve or even develop straightness;
• develop the flexion of all the joints of the inside hind leg and put the horse on the haunch on the shortened side;
• develop the elevation of the neck.
Performing these transitions alternately on the right and the left rein, collects the horse little by little, one half at a time so to speak, in the constant search for symmetry, the ultimate proof of straightness.

Execution

• Draw the horse's attention before every transition by asking for the yielding of the jaw with the inside rein.
• In downwards transitions, stretch up through the upper part of the body and transfer more weight to the hindquarters.
• Invite the horse to lighten the forehand, possibly by means of demi-arrêts on the outside rein.
• With the inside leg at the girth, maintain the bend and the activity of the inside hind leg.
• Channel the hindquarters with the help of the wall and the outside leg acting behind the girth.

Transitions on the circle in travers position (on three tracks)

Because the progressive rotation of the forehand around the haunches relieves weight from the forehand and loads the hindquarters, this position also simultaneously promotes collection and the development of transitions.

Execution

• Prepare the horse for the transition by asking for the yielding of the jaw with the inside rein.
• With the outside rein, keep the forehand on the circle and ask the horse to raise his neck.
• Stretch up through the upper body and increase the load on the inside haunch, above all in downwards transitions.
• With the inside leg acting at the girth, maintain the bend and preserve the activity of the gait.
• With the outside leg acting behind the girth, maintain the angle of displacement and preserve the forward motion.

Examples of transitions

In shoulder-in position on a straight line or in travers position:
• At the walk:
Shorten the walk and perform a halt. Begin the walk again, etc.
• At the trot:
Shorten the trot → walk → trot, etc.
Collect the trot → halt → collected trot, etc.
• At the canter:
Shorten the canter → trot → canter, etc.
Collect the canter → walk → canter, etc.
Collect the canter → walk → halt, →
collected canter, etc.

The more fluid and energetic these transitions become and the more often they succeed, the more the horse's suppleness, impulsion and balance improve – the more it begins to collect. Gradually, the same transitions can be performed on a single track, firstly on the circle, then on a straight line.

Frequent repetition of closer together transitions between a few strides of canter, halt, canter contribute as much to an energetic walk as to a canter that is 'écouté': on the haunches, springy and vibrant. The frequent repetition of closer and closer trot, halt, trot transitions serves to bring the horse to a better balance at the trot, as well as making the halts livelier. Thus, one can put Nuno Oliveira's recommendation into practice: 'The horse should not halt the trot, but trot the halt …'.

Rein-back

A rein-back that is useful for schooling has requirements that go well beyond a utilitarian 'reverse gear'. Firstly, the negative forms of this practise must be identified and rejected because rein-back, depending on how it is performed, can be the best as well as the most damaging of all exercises.

The horse that hardens or even hollows his back pushes backwards with his forelegs. He drops his hocks well out behind and takes long, rushed, non-diagonalised strides. He elongates his base of support and reverses by 'leaning back'. A horse that hollows his top line and comes above the bit ends up refusing to back or even rearing – from pain or lack of understanding for which only the rider is responsible.

Conditions

The horse must show sufficient quality of mise en main and straightness that the rider is able to transfer weight to the rear and channel the hindquarters. In short, he must be confirmed in the shoulder-in on both reins.

Definition

The horse must go back straight, taking slow, regular, diagonalised steps. Correct rein-back assumes a reversal of the mechanism of locomotion.

Table 5

Forward movement	Rein-back
• Upper body sitting back • Engaged seat • Legs active at the girth • Fingers open	• Upper body leaning slightly forward • Light seat • Legs passive and behind the girth • Intermittent closing of the fingers
The rider brings the horse 'in front' of himself	The rider brings the horse 'behind' himself
'Legs without hand'	'Hand without legs'

Instead of pushing forwards when the hind leg comes ahead of the vertical, the horse now pulls himself to the rear with the hind leg behind the vertical. This means that all the muscles of the abdominal belt are involved. In order that these muscles can contract efficiently, their antagonists, the back muscles, must yield and lengthen. One can easily deduce the necessary aids.

Principle

The rider must do everything he can to relieve weight from the horse's back, on the one hand, and to be understood, on the other.

Relieving the back: stretching the long back muscles is guaranteed only by neck extension. It cannot therefore be a question of raising the horse's neck under the pretext of shifting weight to the rear. For same reason, the rider leaning back would serve only to load the horse's lumbar spine and to push it down. One must, therefore, bend forwards a little and sit with a very slight fork seat to relieve the horse's back.

Making oneself understood: all in all, common sense dictates that the aids for rein-back must be exactly the opposite of those for forwards movement (table 5).

Observations

Assuming a possible phase of schooling in-hand for braced or resisting horses, all of them very quickly come to understand this clear language, which is based on clearly distinguished aids and requires a minimum of force.

By contrast, the widespread notion that the horse 'must' rein-back thanks to legs that 'push' against a 'resisting' hand so that the impulsion virtually 'bounces off' the bit is extremely odd. Indeed, such a conception can only lead the rider to conclude that not only is this sort of rein-back achieved by compression, but it causes the horse the greatest confusion with regard to the forwards driving effect of the legs. Nothing is more damaging than to risk the obedience to the legs in such a pointless fashion. Because these methods represent 'playing with fire' to such a degree, one is consistently encouraged to limit oneself to the three, four or five steps required in dressage tests. Under these circumstances, anyone with real knowledge would say it would be best to avoid backing altogether.

Uses and application

Properly understood, that is, without opposition of the aids, an elementary form of rein-back can be inserted very early into the course of training. From then on it provides an early and irreplaceable means of achieving direct flexion of the lumbar spine. If rein-back has a gymnastic value, there is no reason to limit it to some symbolic steps – on the contrary, everything indicates one should gradually extend the periods of rein-back.

Straightness: the horse that is naturally bent to the left is naturally inclined to avoid longitudinal flexion of his lumbar spine by displacing his hindquarters to the left. In spite of the limitations of the walls, he will rein-back by deviating his hindquarters to the inside on the left rein, while on the right rein the forehand comes inwards and the hindquarters are pushed out to the wall. The rider must therefore constantly take care when backing to maintain the forehand in front of the haunches with the right indirect rein and by sitting with his weight to the left.

If the horse is familiar with reining-back, one can even perform it on circles. Backing to the right, bent to the right in other words, shortens the base of support of the left diagonal pair considerably thanks to the increased engagement of the right hind leg. To achieve this, the rider must only ask for the movement with a right bend and the right indirect rein to bring the horse more onto his left shoulder, leave his the right leg at the girth and shift the hindquarters to the right by repeated requests of the left leg. The old French masters called this: 'Foule en arrière'. This work complements the flexion of the hindquarters and makes a major contribution to straightening.

One hears everywhere that reining-back destroys obedience to the leg and must therefore be done only rarely. Quite the contrary: if the rider asks for it frequently, without opposing the aids and goes forward immediately afterwards every time with an energetic trot, then backing becomes, psychologically, a factor of increased impulsion. Here we see yet again the power of the formula 'hand without legs, legs without hand'.

It is obvious that a horse that leans on the reins and is heavy on the forehand will benefit much more in terms of légèreté and impulsion from frequent transitions between trot and rein-back than if he is worked at a trot while compressed between hand and leg. Rein-back done badly is always too much. Rein-back done well is never too much.

Perfection of rein-back

Once a horse is confirmed in correct rein back one can begin to practise collected rein back. One can then use the advantages of this exercise to increase the longitudinal flexion of the lumbar spine and the activity of the hindquarters.

Execution

If the horse is accustomed to rein-back with a discreet forwards movement of the rider's shoulders and drawing back of the legs, the rider can now use short, repeated touches of the latter. There may be, at most, a short hesitation on the part of the horse but no misunderstanding. There can be no mistake with the aids because the drawn-back position of the legs is quite distinct form the one that signifies 'forwards'.

Just as the hand 'filters' the forwards movement, the legs can 'filter' the backwards steps, so that they become at the same time lively and shorter – that is, collected. If necessary, in order to be better understood and to increase the active flexing of the entire hindquarters, the rider can accompany the leg aids with simultaneous and light touches of two whips on the horse's haunches. Indirectly, via the request with two whips or the simultaneous effect of both spurs, the rider can soon obtain the desired result with only the leg aids. With this action the rider develops the means to shorten the horse and to achieve lively, diagonal steps. This is particularly useful with horses that have a stiff or sagging back and with those that back by dragging their feet or hurrying.

Of course, the horse must advance in sparkling fashion after backing on the mere return of the legs to their normal position. In collected rein-back, the rider can now encourage increased elevation of the neck since there is no danger in transferring weight onto flexed haunches and active hind legs.

High School transitions

Once the horse is confirmed in the preceding stages, it has all the necessary abilities (suppleness, impulsion, straightness) to attempt the most difficult transitions on a straight line.

By frequently asking for collected rein-back, the rider has been able to explain to the horse the significance of drawing his legs back: they activate the hindquarters, engage the hind legs under the mass and set the horse on his haunches. Thus he can arbitrarily collect any gait and attempt any transition under optimum conditions.

Case study

Within a gait: if the rider does not change his balance but acts by drawing his legs back, the horse increases his activity without quickening or slowing.

The suspension phase becomes longer and the gait more collected. If the rider animates the steps by drawing his legs back but sits back slightly and holds with the hand at the same time, the horse collects and shortens the gait, eventually coming to a halt.

The horse having halted, if the rider inclines his upper body imperceptibly forwards, the horse begins to back. If the rider brings his upper body and legs back into alignment with the seat, the horse must advance immediately, at the walk, trot or canter depending on the aids employed.

Uses and applications

If the rider proceeds in such a way using clear, differentiated, alternated and judiciously combined aids, he develops the means to extend and perfect the entire range of transitions.

Through logical, systematic work the horse becomes finer and lighter to the aids, gains in suppleness and mobility and can eventually alternate from the trot or canter to rein-back and vice versa without any 'dead point'. This corresponds to a degree of collection that opens the doorway to the High School airs.

It also underlines a fundamental reciprocal relationship in equitation:

**the more one mobilises a horse,
the more he collects;
the more he collects,
the more he becomes mobile.**

Should it be necessary, this formula confirms once again the essential role that transitions play in the schooling of collection – presuming, of course, that the horse is not compressed by aids used in opposition.

Finally, we should note that longitudinal strength and flexibility are also promoted very much by correct jumping and judicious use of varied terrain: lengthening on slightly rising ground; shortening, halting and reining-back on downward slopes.

A horse in the media

Odin is one of those horses who, like some actors or dancers, especially impress the spectator on account of a charisma that lends an inexplicable charm to their presentations.

Nevertheless, one can offer some reasons as to why this horse was held in such high esteem by photographers and cameramen. Apart from the fact that he was often in the foreground as a soloist, one must admit that greys catch and reflect the light more than other horses. Experts have an eye for it. The photographer, Alain Laurioux, always kept a place of honour in his exhibits for Odin, and even published three souvenir posters that became best sellers at the National Riding School.

In addition, not only was Odin kept entire, he always displayed the behaviour of a dominant stallion which, while it indeed causes some serious obedience problems, also gives him an uncommon presence and radiance. All in all, it is virtually impossible for him to remain unnoticed; his strong personality gives his work a particular cachet that touches the spectator. It would have been a crime to castrate this horse – yet God knows how often I was advised to do so!

There was hardly a national or foreign newspaper report on the performances of the Cadre Noir without a photo of Odin under saddle or in long reins. He was also honoured by numerous specialist publications. In France he was often to be seen in Cheval magazine or L'Éperon. He also appeared in Italy in Cavallo magazine, in Switzerland in the magazine Pegasus, in Belgium in Le Monde Équestre and in the USA in Equus. He even had the honour of being on the cover of The Horse magazine in Australia and Saint Georg in Germany.

To finish with the written press, Odin took pride of place in the title picture of the book Emploi des longues rênes. This work appeared of course in French, but also in English (Long Reining, The Saumur Method), German and Japanese. In addition, a video tape is available on the same subject in German.

When the director Serge Bourguignon made a film about the Cadre Noir, entitled 'Variations sur airs et allures' ('Variations on airs and gaits'), for the National Riding School, he also allocated a significant section to Odin. Thus he was filmed on the banks of the Loire, in front of the château de Saumur and in the riding hall of the School.

Television cameras also never tired of following him.

Pesade in front of the château de Saumur

Partnerland der Equitana 91

Franzosen schicken ihre Gold-Stars

EQUITANA-International: Insgesamt 24 Länder präsentieren sich auf der EQUITANA 91. Dabei hat jede Nation ihre eigene Tradition etwa in der Entwicklung der Zucht, des Freizeitreitens oder des Pferdesports. EQUITANA HEUTE stellt in einer Serie die bedeutendsten Pferde-Länder(gruppen) vor. Der erste Teil gilt dem diesjährigen Partnerland Frankreich, das mit eindrucksvollem Programm die Messetage gestalten wird. Bonjour, la France!

Vor besonders eindrucksvoller Kulisse präsentiert sich das diesjährige Partnerland Frankreich auf der EQUITANA 91. Die 25 französischen Aussteller wohnen in einem eigenen „Dorf" in Halle 1, das den Namen „Chevaux de France" trägt. Neben einem Präsentationsring ist darin auch ein Restaurant eingerichtet.

Frankreich ist ohne Zweifel ein Pferdeland par excellence. Zur Zeit werden zwischen Ärmelkanal und Mittelmeerküste etwa 332 000 Pferde und 500 000 Reiter gezählt. Durch die großen sportlichen Erfolge hat Reiten einen hohen gesellschaftlichen Stellenwert erreicht. Nicht nur die Engländer sind eine wettbegeisterte Nation. Zumindest wenn es um Pferde geht, sitzt den Franzosen das Geld ebenso locker. Auf den 275 französischen Rennbahnen finden pro Jahr etwa 15 500 Rennen statt. Am Totalisator werden dabei rund 33 Milliarden Francs (!) umgesetzt. Die Gewinne daraus fließen dem Sport und der Zucht indirekt wieder zu. Sie stellen einen wichtigen Eckpfeiler für den sportlichen Erfolg dar. Die Nummer eins unter den Pferdesportarten ist das Springreiten, erläuterte Nationaltrainer Patrick Caron kürzlich in einem Interview mit der EQUITANA-HEUTE. Nach den Erfolgen von Stockholm werde es nun aber unmöglich sein, hier noch besser zu werden.

Das „Geheimnis des französischen Modells", so Caron, liege in der Vielseitigkeit des Angebotes, die vor allem durch die Haras Nationaux, die Nationalgestüte, gesichert werde. Wichtig sei ferner, daß gute Pferde nicht ins Ausland verkauft werden dürften.

In seinem Grußwort an die Gäste der EQUITANA 91 verweist der Geschäftsführer der

Die Glocke — Westfalen

Begeisternde Premiere

Majestätische Reitkunst vom Cadre Noir de Saumur

Von NICOLETTE FÜCHTENKORT

Die Arbeit an der Doppellonge: Monsieur Karl, Bereiter der französischen Elitereittruppe „Cadre Noir de Saumur", führte dem begeisterten Publikum in der Halle Münsterland bei der Premierenvorstellung den mächtigen Schimmel ... Befreit vom Gewicht des Reiters bekamen die Bewegungen des Pferdes eine ...

Rencontre avec Philippe Karl Ecuyer au Cadre Noir

un point de vue particulier sur le dressage moderne

Eröffnet mit einem Cadre Noir, das in einer Aufführungsreihe schulen der der Halle mierenvor...

Mit stehender schiedete Cadre Noir, das in einer tungsreihe schulen der der Halle mierenvor...

La magie d'un Carrousel nocturne

14 juillet exceptionnel à Saumur cette année : on y présentera pour la première fois un carrousel de nuit. Un événement marqué par la présence du ministre des Sports, Roger Bambuck, et d'une illustre marraine : la comédienne Julie Arnold.

Des diplomates, des politiques, des patrons de l'industrie et des artistes sont attendus pour ce spectacle totalement inédit et que la nuit rendra magique. Des milliers de spectateurs sur les tribunes et sur la carrière du Chardonnet, cent chevaux et autant de cavaliers, ceux du Cadre noir en costume historique (notre photo) ou traditionnel et ceux de l'École de l'arme blindée cavalerie. Soit un spectacle de haute école et de jeux équestres dans une mise en scène originale.

(Photo CO)
Maine-et-Loire

MIDI FERIA

Elégance

Odin aux longues rênes

Cheval Magazine Déc-90

Le Cadre Noir sur le sable des arènes hier et à nouveau ce soir

Emotion au pas de Carrousel

Eclaboussés de lumière, écuyers et chevaux offrent une symphonie de rêve qui associe élégance, légèreté et harmonie. Quand le rêve devient réalité

• Le Cadre Noir assure la pérennité des principes hérités des plus grands noms de l'histoire de la cavalerie. Hier soir, sur le sable des arènes, les vingt « Dieux » menés par leur chef, le colonel Christian Cardé – appelé « Grand Dieu » –, ont plongé le public dans une émotion hors du commun en lui offrant une équitation d'une pureté classique dans laquelle s'associaient étroitement élégance, légèreté, discrétion des aides et harmonie de l'ensemble.

Le décor et le lieu servaient merveilleusement à la gloire de l'homme et de sa plus noble conquête, parce que si le Cadre Noir est le fer de lance du patrimoine équestre français, il sait aussi s'adapter à des publics divers, en raison d'une scénographie confiée à des professionnels du spectacle.

Pour en être académique, l'équitation qui restitue aux chevaux présentés les attitudes qui sont les leurs en li-

Philippe Karl présente, lors des spectacles du Cadre Noir, son andalou Odin aux airs d'école classique. Ici, la pesade. (Ph. E.N.E.A. Laurioux)

AVEC LE SPECTACLE EN FER DE LANCE

Les chevaux rehaussent de leur beauté, de leur énergie, quantité de spectacles à travers le monde. Des spectacles aux formes multiples. Des spectacles qui gomment peu à peu l'image d'austérité attachée à l'équitation. Tout en haut de l'échelle, parce que leur maîtrise de l'art équestre est la plus grande, deux grandes maisons se produisent régulièrement : l'Ecole espagnole de Vienne et le Cadre Noir. Garantes du respect de la tradition et de sa qualité, elles dominent la scène internationale de l'équitation académique.

Le Cadre Noir a proposé un spectacle inédit à Bercy en 1995 avec la cantatrice Julia Migenes. -Ph.Jean Bihard/Studio FEP

VENDREDI SOIR SUR TF1

pétitions par les ambassadeurs involontaires que sont les frères Pinto. Elle ne s'est pas encore produite sur une scène aussi imposante que celle du Palais omnisport de Paris-Bercy.
Toutes ces écoles relayées par des formations plus locales, comme celle de Kladrub en Tchéquie ou celle des éleveurs du Hanovre, ou plus jeunes, comme l'Académie

Le Cadre Noir chez Sabatier

AUSBILDUNG

Im Gespräch mit Philippe Karl vom Cadre Noir in Saumur

1825 gibt es im französischen Saumur an der Loire königliche Kavallerieschule. Um die Bereiter der Schule gegenüber anderen militärischen Ausbildern herauszuheben, wurden sie nach ihrer eleganten schwarzen Uniform als «Cadre Noir» bezeichnet. Sie bildeten etwa 30 Jahre lang den Lehrkörper der Kavallerieschule Saumur.

die Kavallerie keine militärische Bedeutung mehr wechselte auch die Verantwortung für das Cadre Noir vom Verteidigungsministerium in die Zuständigkeit des Ministeriums für Jugend und Sport. 1972 wurde in Saumur die staatliche Reitschule Ecole Nationale d'Equitation gegründet, in welcher die Bereiter des Cadre Noir sowohl in der Reitlehrerausbildung als auch in der Förderung

Work at the canter

Canter departs

Photographs and slow motion filming have shown that the sequence of motion differs significantly depending on whether the horse takes the canter from the trot or from the walk.

From the trot: the left-lead canter begins with disassociation and opening of the left diagonal leg pair in anticipation of the loading of the left foreleg.

From the walk: the left-lead canter is initiated by the formation of a shortened right diagonal leg pair, in anticipation of the loading of the left hind leg.

One can see from this that, from the trot, the horse takes the canter by 'losing his balance' and falling onto his forehand while, from the walk, he takes the canter by 'preserving his balance' on his haunches. The horse must first learn the canter depart from the trot before perfecting it as soon as possible from the walk.

The aids for the canter depart

This is also a matter of establishing some conventions. These will be more easily understood the more they derive from the characteristics of this gait.

In the canter, one lateral pair of legs spends approximately two thirds of the time in front of the other. It is an asymmetrical, rocking gait. The rocking movement is facilitated by an extended neck. The rider can favour the canter depart on a certain lead, the right for example, if the aids:
• limit (overload) the range of movement of the left lateral leg pair as much as possible;
• encourage (relieve and activate) the range of motion of the right lateral leg pair.
• If necessary, give the horse an oblique posture, so that the right leg pair reaches in front of the left pair. This should be achieved not by displacing the hindquarters to the right, but by shifting the forehand to the left. The straightness of later canter departs depends on this condition.

Canter departs from the trot

On the circle
This is the easiest case, because the horse spontaneously takes the lead on the inside leg.

The aids:
• Right bend and right indirect rein which pushes the shoulders to the left.
• Sit to the left
• Left leg behind the girth to prevent any displacement of the hindquarters.
• Right leg active at the girth.

On a loop
In principle, any curve is favourable, but the figure that offers the greatest variation and range of possibilities is the loop. The rider asks for the canter after the change of direction on the second sloping line of the figure.

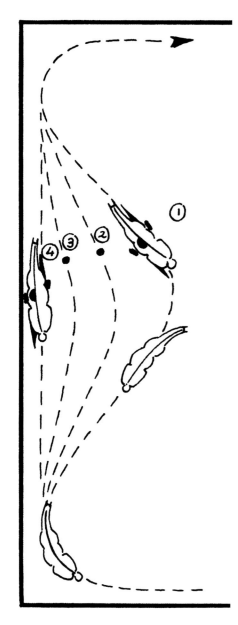

Teaching the canter depart on a loop

In the beginning one rides a wide loop that requires a clear turn. Gradually, one can use a less pronounced loop. In the end, the loop line is only a hint and the horse takes the canter on a straight line without leaving the track.

Canter departs from the walk

Once the canter depart from the trot is confirmed on both reins, there should be no problem in obtaining it with the same aids from the walk.

On the circle
With a horse that is naturally bent to the left.
Left-lead canter
Taking the canter on the left lead is natural for this horse and is easy for him, because he tends to overload his right shoulder, bring his hindquarters to the inside, engage his left hind leg and push with the right hind leg, everything one needs for the left-lead canter.
Right-lead canter
Canter on the right lead is less natural and requires thorough preparation. Use a clear right bend and right indirect rein to bring more weight on the left shoulder by enlarging the circle. The rider sits to the left. The hindquarters are channelled by the left leg behind the girth. Engagement of the right hind leg is encouraged by the action of the rider's right leg at the girth.

On a straight line
The horse should gradually be brought to take the canter on a straight line through a careful progression and preparation that puts it into a favourable balance.

Principles
If we take the case of the depart to the right-lead canter: as we know, the maximum loading of the left lateral leg pair is achieved by a turn to the left in counter-bend. Therefore, the rider

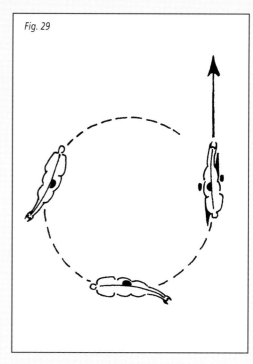

Using the circle to prepare for canter departs on a straight line

must prepare the horse on curves to the left with counter-bend (circles, demi-voltes, loops) and ask for the canter at the moment he leaves the curve on a tangent.

The aids
There is one difference that must be emphasised in contrast to canter departs from the trot: we know that taking the canter from the walk implies the 'preservation of balance'. From this, it follows that the rider must sit not only to the outside, but also to the rear in order to fix the outside haunch and to favour even more the engagement of the inside hind leg which initiates the first canter stride.

Canter departs on the track

To achieve very successful and straight canter departs on a straight line it is sensible, in the beginning at least, to adapt the preparation and the aids to the desired lead leg. Irrespective of whether the horse should canter on the inside lead or the outside lead, the following precautions should be observed:

Left-lead canter:
Limit the risk of the horse going crooked.
• Position the horse in a shallow left shoulder-in (shoulder-fore).
• Little or no left bend.
• Sit with the weight towards the right haunch.
• The right leg rests lightly against the horse behind the girth.
• The left leg works at the girth to align the left hind leg and then activate the departure.

Right-lead canter:
Ensure a straight and frank departure.
• Place the horse in the 'bent-straight' position.
• Bend to the right and right indirect rein to ensure the alignment of the left lateral leg pair.
• Sit with the weight clearly towards the left haunch.
• Left leg behind the girth, vigilant, ready to prevent any escape of the left hind leg.
• Right leg works actively at the girth to produce a distinct engagement of the right hind leg.

Bit by bit, the canter departs become more reliable, more symmetrical and straighter. On the outside lead, the rider benefits from the guidance of the walls, particularly on the right rein.

Counter-canter

This specialist term designates the deliberate canter on the outside lead. For reasons of clarity and consistency, we distinguish it from the canter on the 'wrong' lead, by which we mean the horse has made a mistake. This differentiation is justified; how can one call something that is a useful exercise 'wrong'?

The corresponding descriptions are, therefore: 'canter – counter-canter' and 'correct lead – wrong lead'.

Justification of the counter-canter

The execution of curves in counter-canter is one of the obligatory exercises in numerous dressage tests. The exercise is often justified by the argument that it 'improves the horse's balance'.

Common sense contradicts this assertion through the following three observations:

Whether running free or on the lunge, horses spontaneously canter on the inside lead because they find their optimum balance by doing so. The rider upon whom a young horse forces the canter on the 'wrong' leg quickly feels the unease and imbalance that accompanies it.

A horse that deliberately insists on cantering on the 'wrong' (outside) lead generally does so only on one rein (on the right rein if it is naturally bent to the left). No rider trying out a young horse would be happy about this, because it reveals a distinctive asymmetry and, in truth, a lack of balance!

Horses only change of their own accord to the canter on the outside lead leg when they find themselves going too quickly on a circle (on the lunge, for example). Because of the centrifugal forces created, the hindquarters break away, the horse positions himself at an angle to the outside and becomes disunited or canters on the outside lead because of the 'loss of balance'. In this way, in an extreme case the horse refuses to turn.

Conclusion
Far from improving the horse's balance, the counter-canter makes it more difficult. This is precisely why the horse doesn't do it himself. Really the counter-canter serves to confirm the canter on a given lead, to ensure that one can change the lead without risking the horse becoming restless or tense, going disunited or changing without the request. That is already asking a lot. Thus the value of counter-canter is as a preparation and indispensable supplement to learning the flying change.

The aids for counter-canter

Due to fear of a mistake – going disunited or a change that was not asked for – the counter-canter is often executed as follows: bend to the outside of the track (to the left, for example), under the pretext of maintaining the canter on the desired lead and press with the right leg behind the girth to prevent any possible change of lead.

The inevitable consequence of using the aids in this way is that the horse produces a cramped canter (the outside, left, shoulder is restrained) with the haunches angled to the outside. All in all, the gait is lifeless, shortened and on the forehand. The expected improvement in balance remains nothing but an illusion. Performed like this, the counter-canter only causes problems that one should not inflict on either oneself or the horse.

Typical application of the aids in counter-canter

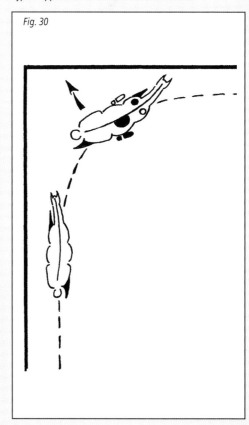

Fig. 30

Deduced aids

If we take as the most convincing example counter-canter on the right rein (left leg leading) with a horse that is naturally bent to the left: our study of the horse's movement has revealed that the horse cantering freely on the left lead on a straight line bends his head and neck to the right each stride in order to pull his left shoulder forwards. If he should now follow a curve to the right, the left shoulder (on the outside of the curve) has to travel even further. Only bending to the right, which stretches and elongates the left side of the neck, encourages this movement. Logically, then, one should bend to the inside of the track.

The rider sits with his weight clearly towards the right, because the horse is turning in this direction and the outside lateral leg pair needs more freedom to move since it describes the bigger arc. It is preferable to maintain the left-lead canter with the left leg at the girth, which encourages the engagement of the left hind leg, rather than the right leg behind the girth, which would only encourage any tendency to go crooked. Finally, since straightness is particularly crucial to this exercise, the rider can send the shoulders to the left with the aid of the bend to the right and the associated right indirect rein. If the horse tries to traverse, the shoulders can be put back in front of the haunches by enlarging the circle.

Therefore: the bend must correspond to the ridden line and not to the lead leg on which the horse canters. The light, relaxed canter that this practice enables allows one to achieve large circles quite early on, which can then be reduced bit by bit with the horse always straight.

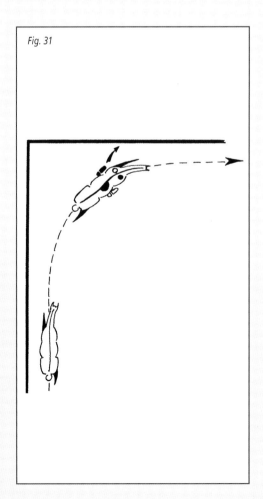

Fig. 31

Correct application of the aids in counter-canter

Impact

With the same tempo and on the same circle, the horse must take longer strides on the outside lead than on the inside lead. One can see, therefore, that the counter-canter can serve to extend the canter strides – on condition, of course, that one rides well forward on a large circle with the neck extended and bent to the inside.

Properly understood, the counter-canter is an effective means of correction. With a horse that is naturally bent to the left, it promotes the range of motion of the shoulders on the right rein and the range of motion of the hindquarters on the left rein. Used in this way, it is also an excellent preparation before learning flying lead changes, since it teaches the horse that neither a change of rein nor a change of bend necessarily signify a change of lead but rather 'amplitude'. Thus, this work develops at the same time a guarantee against premature or unintentional changes and that the changes can be achieved with optimal stride length from the outset.

Flying changes

Colonel Wattel was famous for his humorous remarks, for example: 'How nice this School would be, if only it didn't have any pupils!', or 'To teach a horse the passage, one must get up early!' Two of his remarks haunted me during a certain phase of Odin's education: 'How do I ask for the flying change? I think it and that's enough' and 'I have known horses which have never learned the flying change.'

As well as revealing the sensitivity, wit and absolute sincerity of this noteworthy equestrian personality, these statements also indicate, that, technically, flying changes can be the most natural exercise for one horse, and the most invincible difficulty for another.

Since Odin generally belonged in the second category, he required detailed study and much perseverance, the fruit of which is described below.

Analysis of flying changes

What is a flying change?
In simple terms, one could say it is a canter depart from the canter – straight, without loss of impulsion and initiated by inversion of the strides of the hind legs. To tackle them seriously, the horse must be confirmed in lateral work and in canter departs from the walk on both reins, on straight lines as well as on the circle, as well as in the counter-canter.

Conditions that favour the flying change

Of all the exercises to which one submits the horse, the flying change of lead is the only one that cannot be demanded from the outset. There is necessarily a certain day and a certain time when the rider asks for 'the first' lead change.

However good the preparation may have been, the horse is often unsettled at the beginning because the lead change happens in a split second – all the more so if he is more sensitive or if the exercise does not correspond to his natural disposition. In this case one may leave nothing to chance, study the phenomenon in detail and derive the critical requirements and consequently the appropriate aids.

Tempo and cadence

The inversion of the legs can occur only while the limbs are off the ground – during the suspension phase. The longer this is, the more time the horse has to perform the change (one only needs to hop along oneself while dragging a foot to understand this). This explains why flying changes are easy for horses that have a naturally long and cadenced canter – even if they are stiff and rather heavy to the aids. There are many that can easily perform tempi-changes, although they are otherwise mediocre, above all in collection. It is no coincidence that tempi-changes appeared and became part of equestrianism in the nineteenth century. That epoch favoured 'rectangular' horses with extended gaits, in particular the English Thoroughbred.

With less gifted horses one must develop an extended suspension phase. This is possible if one associates quite a high tempo with a certain degree of collection. In other words one must ride 'forwards' enough to achieve the necessary amplitude with enough activity to generate rebound. Rushing is the main enemy of the flying change.

Balance, posture

During a correct flying change, the reversal of the movement within the same canter stride must begin with the hind legs and be completed with the forelegs. Otherwise one says that the horse changes 'late behind'.

To favour changing with the hind legs first, it is useful to relieve them and, therefore, let the horse canter in an extended posture. The low posture of the head relieves the croup, releases and rounds the back – all of which amplify the rocking movement and improve stride length and rebound even further.

Execution

To perform a flying change from the left lead to the right, the left hind foot touches the ground twice in succession, while the touchdown of the right hind is delayed. The same applies to the left forefoot which touches down twice, while the right fore remains in the air. It follows, then, that the rider must relieve the right side so that the horse can prolong and lengthen its suspension phase – and that he must load the left side so that the horse shortens its movements and anticipates returning to the ground. The rider obtains the necessary transfer of weight to the left shoulder by bending the neck to the right in association with a right indirect rein effect.

He assists further by sitting with his weight to the left and, because the change begins with the hindquarters, in the direction of the left haunch in such a way as to shorten the suspension phase of the left hind leg. Since the flying change corresponds to a change of bend, the rider activates it by inverting the position of his legs. The left leg is applied behind the girth while the right leg slides forward to the girth.

Because the lead change begins with the left hind leg, the horse can only react to the leg aid after the moment when that leg leaves the ground. This corresponds to the end of the second phase of the canter stride before the horse rocks his weight onto his left foreleg. If one takes into consideration the necessary reaction time, the rider must use his aids at the beginning of the second phase of the canter stride, just as the diagonal leg pair lands. If the horse is 'prewarned' in this way, one can avoid jerky or hopping changes.

One could say that a flying change from the left to the right means causing the horse to 'yield' and lengthen his left side. It is by resisting this lengthening, among other factors, that the horse that is naturally bent to the left delays the change from the left to the right by reducing the amplitude or, in the worst case, changing late behind.

Straightness – position

A correct flying lead change is executed absolutely straight. If this exercise is especially difficult for a horse he will commit faults that are closely related to his innate asymmetry. If naturally bent to the left, one sees the following.

From right lead to left:
On the right lead, the horse carries his right lateral leg pair ahead of the left. During the change, his left lateral leg pair must begin to reach out in front of the right, namely during the suspension phase.

Always ready to bend to the left, and to support his weight on the right diagonal leg pair, the horse will instinctively be happy to change from the right lead to the left, but will often go crooked.

From left lead to right:
If the horse senses a change coming and displaces his left hind to the outside even a little during the preparation, the shift of the right lateral leg pair ahead of the left is compromised and the engagement of the right hind leg is delayed. The change stride will be cramped at best, or both hind legs may land together. In the worst case the change is late behind.

It follows, then, that to give the best chance of success the change must be prepared from the left to the right by giving the horse a posture which favours having the right leg pair ahead of the left and obliges the left hind leg to leave the ground in the direction of the centre of gravity. These conditions are fulfilled when the rider, while maintaining the left-lead canter, succeeds in placing the shoulders ahead of the left hind leg.

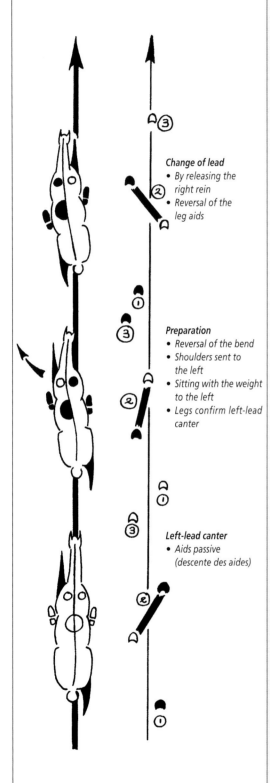

Fig. 32

Change of lead
- By releasing the right rein
- Reversal of the leg aids

Preparation
- Reversal of the bend
- Shoulders sent to the left
- Sitting with the weight to the left
- Legs confirm left-lead canter

Left-lead canter
- Aids passive (descente des aides)

Application of the aids for flying lead changes

From this position – right bend and a slight obliqueness with the tendency to align the right diagonal leg pair; in other words: the principle of half-pass to the right (which one could call, according to Steinbrecht's teachings 'canter position to the right') – the rider has the best chance of executing a perfect lead change. This is the ultimate solution.

Development of schooling the flying change

On the assumption that if one can solve the more difficult problem, one can also solve the easy problem, we will take as an example the more difficult change: the change from the left lead to the right with a horse that is naturally bent to the left.

We will consider two progressions in parallel:
• From the single change to changes in series with a horse that has no particular problems.
• From the most elementary preparations to the most refined means in order to obtain correct changes with a difficult horse.

Summary of the conditions that favour the first changes of lead:
• Extended suspension phase: seeking the best compromise between extension and rebound. Thus: increased activity while going forward.
• Hindquarters unloaded: horse round and carrying his head slightly deeper.
• Increased loading of the left lateral leg pair, more especially the left hind leg. Therefore: right bend, right indirect rein, sitting with the weight towards the left haunch.
• The right leg pair is carried ahead of the left: at a minimum, position the horse so that the left lateral leg pair is aligned with the direction of travel, at a maximum, the right diagonal leg pair.

NB: It should come as no surprise to find once again the overall conditions for useful counter-canter (with bend to the inside of the track) in these recommendations. The one reinforces the other.

Effective solutions

In principle, the rider can best increase the load on the left lateral leg pair through a shift to the left in counter-bend.

Preparation on the circle

When the rider executes a large circle on the left rein with a right bend and right indirect rein, he can place the shoulders ahead of the left haunch on every canter stride.

Ask for the change while leaving the circle: if the seat has achieved a clear weight transfer to the left lateral leg pair, the rider will ask for the change by closing his legs (the left one going back while the right leg goes forward to the girth) at the exact moment he leaves the circle on a tangent.

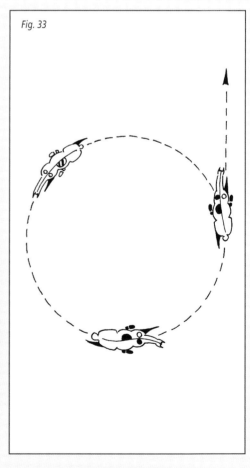

Fig. 33

Using the circle to prepare for flying changes

If the change of lead does not occur, return to a circle to the left and begin the preparation again. On no account should one turn right under the pretext of wanting to make the change easier, since this would soon lead the horse to change lead by 'losing his balance' onto his right shoulder. This would encourage the horse to change late behind. In equitation, the first idea that occurs to the rider is also often the worst.

Loops

Once the correctness of the changes is secured with the help of the circle, they must be confirmed with a preparation that is based on the same principle but in a shortened and simplified form: the loop.

Advantages of this figure

• The loop enables to the rider to ask for the change at the end of part of a curve. Turn to the left to change from the left to the right, and vice versa.

• By progressively flattening the loop the rider gradually approaches the change on a straight line.

• The frequent repetitions required to confirm and perfect flying changes expose the horse to routine and tempt him to begin to anticipate the change. The rider must take care, therefore, to repeat frequently gentle loops on the inside or outside lead without requiring a flying change, so that the figure becomes the focus of routine and not the change.

• Once the horse is familiar with the change on a gentle loop, it becomes possible to execute several of them on the long side and to begin to repeat them and link them closer and closer together.

• Gradually, the rider is able to perform the changes by hinting at the loop. He brings the forehand closer to the wall to change from the outside to the inside lead, and takes away them slightly away from it to change from the inside to the outside lead.

• Eventually, perfectly straight flying changes can be obtained on a straight line merely by the play of the seat and leg aids while constantly seeking their refinement.

Lateral exercises

A solution that can be implemented with horses that turn out to be difficult who, in spite

Fig. 34

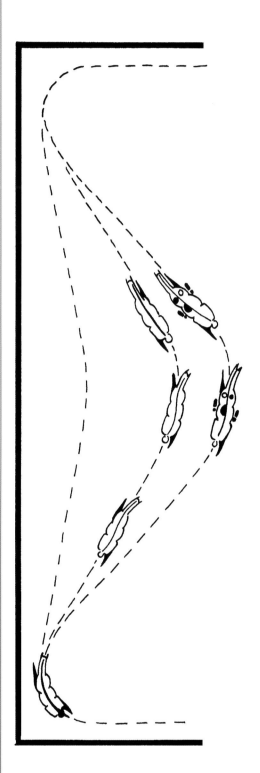
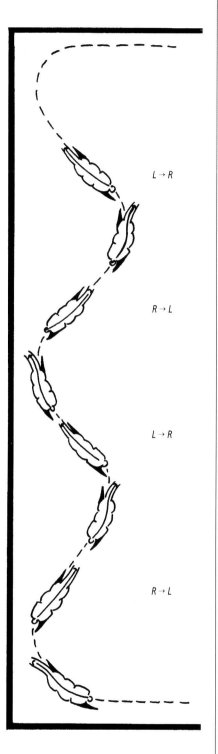

Using loops to develop flying changes

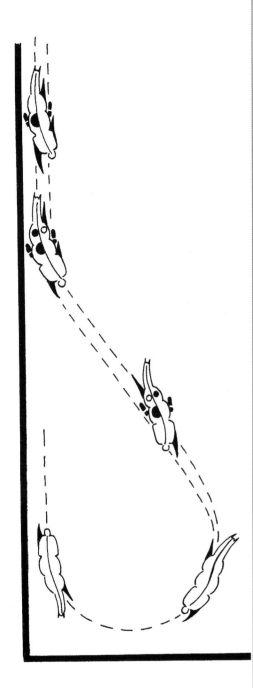

Developing the flying change with a demi-volte on two tracks

of careful preparation, continually refuse the change, run off or change late behind is to perform a demi-volte in counter-bend on two tracks out of a corner. The shoulders must clearly lead the way towards the wall. Thus the horse returns to the track, shoulders first, in 'head to the wall' position. The rider asks for the change at this precise moment, while sitting to the outside and with the left leg behind the girth keeping the haunches off the track.

If there are difficulties, return to the walk in the 'head to the wall' and retake the right-lead canter in this position.

On the circle
From the inside to the outside lead

In absolute extreme cases, the last resort is to ask for the change on the circle from inside to the outside lead. This requires special preparation: one must practise moving the hindquarters to the outside of the circle (renvers) and insist on an absolutely reliable response to the leg nearest the centre of the circle acting behind the girth.

For example, on the left rein:
• While following the circle with the horse bent to the right, insist that the horse responds immediately to the placing of the rider's left leg behind the girth by shifting his hindquarters to the outside and going into renvers, at the walk as well as the trot.
• Take the right-lead canter several times from the walk in renvers position.

In the end, this preparation will enable the rider to insist that the horse move his hindquarters to the outside while cantering on the left lead which, of course, forces a change with the hind legs first.

There are three possible outcomes:
• Either the horse does not change at all because this position makes it impossible for him to change with the forelegs first. This means that he does not yet react enough to the leg behind the girth and the preparation must be repeated again.
• Or the horse responds well to the leg behind the girth, shifts the hindquarters to the right and performs the change, crooked, but without mistake.

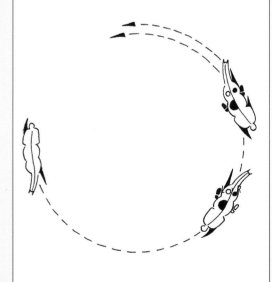

Developing the flying change on the circle

- Sometimes it can be that the horse changes only with his hind legs. Since the right bend limits the range of motion of the horse's right shoulder, he may tend to canter one or several more strides with the left fore leading.

This should not be looked upon as a mistake, but as a valuable success. Praise generously and begin again. The changes will soon become regular all by themselves.

This method is very effective, because it does not allow the horse any possibility of changing in front first.

Impact and areas of application

In the most critical cases this remains the only method that guarantees at least a minimum of success. The difficulty lies in the overall preparation and in the harmony of the rider's aids.

As well as obliging the difficult horse to change with the hind legs first, this system is a very effective way of achieving symmetrical changes. In effect, a horse that changes from the left to the right lead without mistakes but by shortening the canter stride can be corrected by performing the change on a circle on the left rein. Because the horse must change to the outside lead, he cannot help but increase the amplitude of the strides. Once again we see the advantages of the counter-canter.

Changes in series

With a horse that performs single flying changes correctly, that is, calmly, with long strides and straight, one can easily begin to perform changes every five or six strides. From this point, one needs only methodical action and patience to bring the changes closer and closer together, every four, three, two strides. Finally, the rider is ready to tackle tempi-changes.

With a difficult horse, the work is called into question again at each of these stages. Although less severe and less frequent, faults appear again. Thus one must continually attend to two precautions:

- Go back a step to confirm the preceding stage. For example, if the horse makes mistakes when one begins with tempi-changes, practise changes every two strides once again.
- If the horse makes mistakes with the change from the left to the right, return to the work on the circle on the left rein.

Example of schooling changes at every stride

Two changes:

On a circle on the left rein, start with the left-lead canter and ask for two changes as follows:
- Left → right → left. In this manner one secures the more difficult change and ends with the easier one before praising.

Only after that should one tackle the series: right → left → right. Here the horse must perform the more difficult change last.

Three changes in series:

Begin on the right lead and ask for three changes as follows:
- Right → left → right → left

Continue with:
- Left → right → left → right, etc.

Then carry out the whole progression once again on straight line, tirelessly and methodically.

Observations

The value of changes at close intervals, and tempi-changes in particular, merits some discussion. As much as the single flying lead change is unquestionably useful, no matter which discipline the rider pursues, performing changes at every stride resembles 'the conquest of the useless', since, even if one sees aesthetic value in it, it represents above all a difficulty overcome. Before this exercise became accepted as part of equitation, numerous authorities regarded it as a 'trick' of dubious taste. Indeed, experience shows every day that a horse can perform tempi-changes very well, and remain stiff, perfectly unpleasant to ride and barely manoeuvrable – while one that performs piaffe and pirouettes correctly cannot help but be agile and light to the aids. Why?

The explanation is as follows:

- In terms of balance and locomotion collecting exercises place the horse on the hindquarters and 'diagonalise' the gaits.
- The canter is by its nature the least 'diagonal' gait: the trot stride consists of two diagonals, a walk stride likewise contains two, a canter stride, however, only one.
- On the other hand, every change begins, as we have seen, with the dissociation of a diagonal.
- It is as a result of all of these factors that tempi changes produce this very special effect, which General Decarpentry called an 'ambling canter'. Apart from anything else, the rider has the overall sensation of a horse jumping from one lateral leg pair to other.

Normally, any 'lateralisation' of the gaits is undesirable because it is the exact opposite of the 'diagonalisation' that is characteristic of collection.

From that, one can deduce that changes at every stride and collection belong to two different or opposite worlds.

The history of equitation demonstrates this:

- The old masters, who were mainly interested in collection and agility, naturally valued the breeds predisposed to diagonalisation of the gaits, and attached a merely utilitarian value to the single flying change.
- In the course of the nineteenth century, 'galloping Anglomania' led to the rise of the 'blood' horse (as if others had no blood!). As a consequence, under the influence of these rectangular horses who were naturally more on the forehand and less apt for diagonalisation, 'academic' equitation became 'savante' (scientific), moved away from collected airs and invented tempi-changes and various examples of canter on three legs.

This was nothing accidental about it. Has equitation benefited from it, overall? If only one could pose this question without being thought of as a diehard or a heretic.

Odin

A 'God of war', hostile to flying changes

A brainteaser

Hot-blooded, easily excitable and equipped with a mediocre canter, Odin turned out to be especially rebellious over flying changes. In the beginning, even though his education had otherwise progressed very well, I first of all had to stop him getting into a panic with every request.

Once that was achieved, he changed willingly from right to left and left to right; however, he was systematically late behind. I was in despair.

Extenuating circumstances

The only opportunity which had presented itself to prolong Odin's stay at the School was to fulfil his contract in the 'historical presentation', which required a good deal of work: piaffe, passage, pirouettes, pesade etc. Such constraints required the setting of some priorities. Because the flying change was limited to the strictly utilitarian in Pluvinel's time, I was able to spare Odin excessive hassle without impairing the presentations.

Stubbornness

Meanwhile, the error was there still, took root, and I found this gap vexing and was outraged with him. One day, since he could otherwise do the essentials, I decided to tackle the issue. After I had exhausted all the usual means without noticeable progress, I asked some 'experts' to ride Odin and give me their advice. So, Colonel Carde, Philippe Limousin and Alain François tried him and also Catherine Durand and Margit Otto-Crépin – to name a few! Everybody worked with him on flying changes in their own way, with all their experience and their favourite methods.

I observed everything with the greatest attention and drew the following conclusion: the success rate of one or the other was no higher than mine. A pity! The opposite would at least have led me to an explanation, maybe even a possible solution. On the other hand, it absolved me of personal responsibility for the problem. Some consolation!

Everyone was agreed on the diagnosis: the horse found this area very difficult. However, the prescriptions varied tremendously and the prognoses, even for the long-term, were extremely pessimistic.

On reflection, there was something in almost every analysis, so I tried to compile a very logical synthesis and decided to put it into action.

Outside of the presentations, I have worked primarily on flying changes since 1989. At that time, Odin's error rate amounted to at least 80 per cent. Slowly we made ground, step by step, in the course of the months and years, without forgetting the occasional backward steps – Odin could change every two strides in 1992, performed about five tempi-changes in 1994 (the minimum requirement of Grand-Prix-Kür). Between 1996 and 1997 we achieved ten to fifteen tempi-changes, but even today his series of tempi-changes is susceptible to the slightest disturbance and then it is all or nothing.

Altogether I have learned a lot from these difficulties, which only proves that the horse remains the master of the écuyer – and the only pedestal on which one can learn humility.

To conclude this chapter by paying homage to the witty Colonel Wattel, one could say, perhaps: 'For a successful flying change it is not enough to think it. One must also think about it, get up early and even go to bed late.'

Tempi-changes

The death of Monsieur de Saint-Vual

In July 1991, at the end of the Saumur Carrousel, Colonel de Beauregard bade farewell to the School. A celebration dinner reunited the Cadre Noir around him for the last time. Speeches, presents, recollections, emotions – When he finally said his goodbye to us, this extremely reserved man said some simple words to me, and their sincerity and warmth touched me deeply: 'Thank you for everything you have brought to the Manège ...' His recognition will remain forever etched in my mind.

His successor at the head of the Cadre Noir was Colonel Carde. Each Écuyer en chef would like to leave a lasting impression. They achieve this more or less, according to their personality, convictions and the ideas which each brings to his office. But in this very public post there is one siren's call that some cannot resist; to think that one must obliterate the tracks of his predecessor at all costs.

Very soon I had reason for concern about Odin's future. Things came to a head in the spring of 1993. On one of those late mornings when numerous visitors to the School gather in the seating areas while the riders go through their paces under the watchful eye of the écuyer en chef, I had just finished working my horse with some pesades when the Colonel said to me:

'I think I must prohibit you from doing that if there is an audience.'

'I see. Why so, colonel?'

'Because the spectators will want to ask questions', he replied.

There we have it, I thought. So the most important thing is not to seek answers, but to make sure there are no questions.

It was neither the time nor the place to discuss it, but the incident gnawed at me. There was no question of letting the problem fester. That very same afternoon I proceeded to the écuyer en chef's office, absolutely determined to defend my position every step of the way.

'Colonel, I did not understand what you said to me this morning ...'

'Well, now! The spectators won't understand, because you show something very different from the school jumps of the sauteurs ...'

I would have liked to answer: 'You flatter me, Colonel', but it was not the right moment for polemics or confidentiality.

'But, Colonel – correct me if I am mistaken – the pesade is an academic air which was regarded as fundamental by the old masters. That's why I'm trying to restore it within a historical presentation that has been part of all our gala

Monsieur de Saint-Vual at Saumur

performances for many years. There is nothing new in it ... On the other hand, one can divide the visitors to the School into two categories: the complete laymen who have no previous education and will, therefore, not risk asking questions and those who have enough equestrian education that they ask no questions, because they know the answers!'

My counterattack through this advocacy had the desired effect; 'Well! Then, you do as you please!' concluded the Colonel wearily, surprised and short of arguments, partly with tolerance and partly shocked. And we spoke about something else as if nothing had happened.

Nevertheless, I felt I had 'dodged a bullet' and was only partly reassured – quite rightly, because soon a directive was sent to the team responsible for the creation of our presentations, to which I belonged. Essentially, it was an instruction that in future the programme of the galas would be limited to the history of the Cadre Noir from the nineteenth century to the present day.

Round two. It was clear that there was nothing more to discuss and that the 'Protestant Academy' could no longer be a part of the presentations. Monsieur de Saint-Vual would have to die for a second time and Odin would find himself eliminated from presentations where he had always had much success – too much, perhaps!

The five or six members of our small working group were floored, none more than I. I had not yet spoken my last word, however.

After a few days of reflection and bibliographical study to back up my plan, I suggested quite innocently to the Colonel that we create a historical presentation about the origins of the Manège de Saumur, in line with his directives. My abnegation must have seemed genuine, because I was given carte blanche.

Soon afterwards I presented the following solidly documented project: the presentation would focus on the two figures central to the foundation of the Cadre Noir – M. Cordier, the first écuyer en chef, and General L'Hotte, the spiritual heir of his two masters, d'Aure and Baucher. The screenplay invisaged five horses: a sauteur in the pillars, a sauteur and a school horse in-hand plus the horses of L'Hotte and Cordier. Cordier would have to open the presentation to stay faithful to the practices of the time.

I laid my cards on the table, presenting some irrefutable documents. The first came from Capitaine L. Picard's two-volume reference book, Origines de l'école de cavalerie et de ses traditions équestres ('Origins of the cavalry school and its equestrian traditions'). Page 37 concerns an inspection by General Bourbon-Busset, in 1825:

'The Manège de l'École is composed of one hundred and twenty horses of different origin, including seven Spanish horses bought in Bayonne.'

The comparison with the others was apparently not very flattering, because the horses received from the regiments were found to be not very suitable for service at the School. They would have preferred to stick with horses from the Limousin and Navarre, but the minister pointed out that this would be calamitous for French breeding and that they should buy local horses wherever possible.

As we will see, although it obeyed the orders of the minister, the Manège maintained its preference for horses from Limousin and Navarre which were without question the most brilliant in the school exercises.

On page 58:

'In 1828, the school mounts were primarily English horses with docked tails and an average size of 15.2 hh, but for the academic exercises they still recruited horses from the Limousin and Navarre which measured, on average, 15 hh at most.'

The second document came from Traité raisonné d'équitation ('Rational treatise on equitation'), written by Cordier himself and published in 1924. There he defines unambiguously the classical pesade under the title: 'Mézair or half-courbette and from the pesade or courbette in place.'

Conclusion: at that time, the écuyers du Manège were still mounted on Iberian or related horses and still performed the pesade as inherited from the School of Versailles. Now, there was just one single horse at the School that corresponded to and could represent the historical truth: Odin!

The project was approved without any changes, because it was irrefutable. Blessed be the scholarly knowledge of that nice captain L. Picard, instructor at the cavalry school! Thanks to him, Odin, who had barely been thrown out of the servants' entrance along with Monsieur de Saint-Vual, returned again – through the main door and under the saddle of M. Cordier, the first écuyer en chef of the Cadre Noir! Two hundred years of riding tradition on the back of one and the same horse. Such longevity, and what a promotion!

There are some small victories worth enjoying.

I had no regrets about having stood my ground, since the Colonel had no scruples about getting the 'Protestant Academy' out of storage from time to time if it served his purposes. This was the case on two occasions. In April 1994, in Seville, he spotted an excellent opportunity to show the Spaniards the high regard in which our institute holds Iberian horses! And at the Cannes festival in May 1994 he judged that the film world would know how to appreciate this splendid colour picture. Such opportunistic manoeuvres …

In 1997, the écuyer en chef had the excellent idea of organising a colloquium on the subject of collection. Before an audience of riders, advanced amateurs, coaches, judges and journalists the plan was to hold different talks in the auditorium of the School and then move on to some practical presentations in the riding hall.

While the members of the Cadre Noir were not bending over backwards to participate, the écuyer en chef nevertheless needed his School to cut a fine figure in this cultural event and suggested that I take part. Of course, I chose a certain subject very dear to my heart: 'Collection beyond the piaffe' – in other words, the pesade!

In the course of the day I was the only one of the Colonel's écuyers to put theory and practice together. After a talk on the history and technique of riding, which seemed to be appreciated, I presented both of my horses in the hall. With Verdi in-hand and in a cavesson, I discussed teaching the piaffe from the first mobilisations up to the pesade. With Odin I showed the exercise in-hand on the curb, then under saddle. At the end of the presentation the participants of the colloquium gave my horses hearty applause. I was quite satisfied with this little public and official 'redressing of the balance' in front of a professional audience. It purged my horses and my work of a long series of trials and tribulations.

Monsieur Cordier in Münster

Collection

Definition

The concept of collection can be considered from several angles.

The first goes back to its pure utility value in the early days of the cavalry. In effect, the superiority of the more manoeuvrable horse was a vital necessity in close combat using a bladed weapon. Nevertheless, the all-round agility that enables immediate mobility in all directions is only conceivable if one is able to put the horse into an unsteady balance, that is, on a base of support that is shortened from the rear.

The second is one of aesthetic art: it rationalises and codifies the utilitarian aspect of collection. It results from a refinement of morals which led to the pursuit of 'beauty' and the emergence of 'Equestrian Art'. From the time of the Italian Renaissance, academies cultivated collection, no longer just for the needs of combat but equally for the purposes of 'courtly' equitation, in which the horse had to shine with stylised gaits and airs above the ground.

So the concept of collection contains two criteria: one a utilitarian aspect – manoeuvrability, and the other more aesthetic – the stylisation of the gaits. It combines the qualities of the fencer with those of the dancer.

Let's examine the two approaches and the means that they imply.

Mobility

The horse is manoeuvrable in all directions when he finds himself in an unsteady balance which the rider can make him leave or re-establish at will.

So, starting from the natural balance of the ridden horse, how does one achieve this unsteady balance that characterises collection? A simple metaphor can say much more than complicated demonstrations:

• What must one do to give an inert and shapeless lump of plasticine a form that gives it the maximum of mobility in all directions?

• First one must knead the lump softy, so that it becomes malleable. Then, systematically roll it in all directions to form it bit by bit into a ball. We should note that repeated, even skilful compressions of the plasticine by no means lead to a comparable result.

The image is easy to decipher: to collect a horse, one must dissolve his opposition, by de-contracting him – then the horse must be made 'round' to develop his mobility, using the whole range of lateral and longitudinal suppling exercises.

While approaching the unsteady balance we encounter once again the relationship mentioned in the chapter on transitions: while collection improves mobility, it is mobility that leads to collection.

Stylisation of the gaits

Collection makes the movements more elevated and rounder, extends the suspension phase, lends expression and cadence to the gaits and thus leads to their stylised perfection. The old masters spoke of the 'school walk', 'school trot' and 'school canter'.

A well-known aphorism says it all: 'Collection is activity in slowness.' This clarifies the formula illustrated in Table 6. It shows clearly that the degree of collection increases in direct proportion to the degree of activity and in inverse proportion to speed. Collection culminates when maximum energy is deployed in place.

Because collection is not the prerogative of the dressage rider, we will intentionally take jumping as an example. The formula can be applied quite specifically to two cases that the rider encounters if he would like to ride optimally towards big fences.

If the approach to the take-off point is good, the rider maintains the tempo and length of the canter strides but to help the horse elevate his trajectory he will, at the same time, help him re-balance and build up energy to achieve the necessary jumping power. The horse, therefore, approaches the fence at a constant tempo, but with increasing collection (Table 7).

In motor sport, one would say the driver changes down a gear to take a gradient at full speed.

If the rider wants to get closer under the fence to guarantee clearing a massive obstacle, he must first of all develop high impulsion, then shorten the canter strides and reduce the tempo – by transferring weight to the rear without any loss of activity. Thus the horse approaches the obstacle with decreasing stride length and increasing collection (Table 8). We owe the definition and promotion of these famous 'shortening strides' to the educational genius, Jean d'Orgeix.

In motoring, one would say that the driver uses engine braking to slow down while maintaining maximum power.

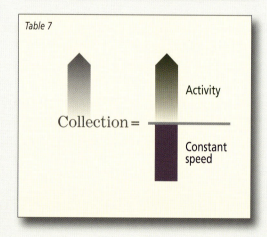
Table 6

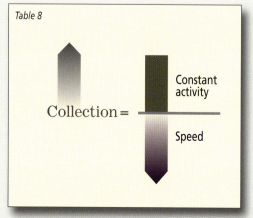
Table 7

Table 8

The above examples show that the rider can collect the horse only to the extent that he has the means to increase activity without accelerating – or slow down without losing activity.

The stylisation of the gaits in légèreté is not compatible with an approach where 'restraining' and 'forwards-driving' aids are used in opposition and which produces horses that are more compressed than collected.

To achieve collection, it is necessary to work on only one variable at a time and to alternate back and forth in order to develop them in parallel but not simultaneously. Only judicious, subtle work on transitions can lead to collection founded on respect of the principle of 'hand without legs, legs without hand' and the pursuit of légèreté. One could summarise the problem like this: collecting a horse means making him 'round', without putting him 'in a spin'.

The piaffe

'I believe that it is the foundation stone of High School.' (Nuno Oliveira)

Principles

To achieve this 'measured', cadenced, springy and majestic trot in place (trot 'écouté', in French) one must, of course, combine perfect balance with a high degree of impulsion – which can be only be achieved with complete lightness to the aids (légèreté). Any attempt to 'put the horse together' with strong aids must be absolutely prohibited. 'Cranking and spanking' only generates resistances and a faulty piaffe.

To achieve the gradual development of diagonalised steps that leads slowly but surely to the piaffe, the rider must combine the following exercises:

• Exercises that engage the hind legs, flex the lumbar spine and put the horse on the

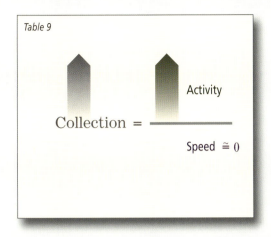

Table 9

$$\text{Collection} = \frac{\text{Activity}}{\text{Speed} \cong 0}$$

haunches in a diagonal gait (collected halts from the trot, rein-back). Improvement of balance and longitudinal flexibility.
• Exercises that test and develop the horse's reactions in all situations (instantaneous and energetic departures to the trot, from the halt as well as from rein-back). Improvement of impulsion.

The use of clearly differentiated aids, applied during systematic training of trot, halt, trot and trot, rein-back, trot transitions enables the rider to improve their quality and increase their frequency.

Once the horse shows enough légèreté and mobility to go from some trot steps to rein-back and back to the trot again without any 'dead spot' he is ready to begin learning the piaffe. Once the rider has developed the activity of the trot and the balance in the rein-back to the extreme, he is able to connect them in short sequences and to make himself understood by the horse.

In effect, thanks to the interplay of these very close transitions, there comes a moment when the horse reins-back with the thought of the depart to the trot and so gathers his forces like a cat ready to pounce, then trots with the thought of the imminent transition to rein-back so is always ready to sit down. Then, the rider must only filter the horse's constant desire to advance out of the rein-back to produce some energetic diagonal steps whereby the horse barely advances. Thus, the first piaffe steps originate from an irrepressible desire to take the trot which the rider can delay for some moments by establishing the appropriate balance.

Variations

The rider must approach these transitions according to the conformation, balance and temperament of his horse.
• If the horse has a tendency to hollow his back, the rider must put him to the piaffe in a posture that is low enough that he stays round and correctly mise en main.
• If the horse tries to bear on the forehand, one must go with a more elevated piaffe.
• If the horse reacts sluggishly and has a tendency to be lazy, one must practise transitions to trot from the halt and from rein-back even more frequently and energetically, without tolerating even the slightest delay.

Under no circumstances must the rider force or maintain the piaffe with the spurs, the whip or an assistant on foot, because the repeated application of strong or punitive aids to these 'steps in place' would serve only to dull the horse even more. On the contrary, the rider develops the essential impulsion by leaving the piaffe with an explosive trot, supported by the whip or spurs as required, at the slightest hint of a drop in energy. In fact, one should praise the horse, not for the piaffe itself, but for the frankness of the departure to the trot to reward forward movement.
• If a keen horse appears feverish with excitement, one should be wary of using his excitability while reinforcing the 'restraining' aids. This would only exaggerate the piaffe and cause resistances. On the contrary, one should begin from a calm walk, then gradually lengthen and prolong the periods of rein-back, before attempting the piaffe. One should interrupt the piaffe at the slightest sign of anxiety by standing absolutely still until calm returns. In extreme cases one can happily fall back on the effet d'ensemble. With such hot-blooded horses one must turn the piaffe into something casual, by rewarding calmness and immobility.

As the horse gains in experience with the piaffe and the associated aids, the rider needs less and less preparation and concentrates increasingly upon the perfection of the exercise. The more the horse improves his impulsion and balance in complete de-contraction, the more his piaffe becomes elevated, in place and sustainable. He 'enjoys his air'.

Conclusions

Work in the piaffe confirms the formula illustrated in Table 9.

While it lacks poetry, the motor sport metaphor is no less appropriate: piaffe can be compared to a hill start. There are two possibilities:
• The driver puts the car in gear, engages the hand brake so as not to roll back and revs the engine to the extreme with the aim of generating power, while letting out the clutch. All in all, he uses and abuses all of the means available. Starting becomes drawn out and laborious: mediocre driving.

This is exactly what happens if the rider tries to bring his horse to piaffe by pushing and pulling. The result is disappointing, even if the horse has the potential of Ferrari.
• The driver engages first gear and revs the engine a little while allowing the clutch to begin to bite. The car is held by the power of the engine and can take off like lightning as soon as the driver releases the clutch: efficient, sports driving.

This is exactly what the rider does if he develops the piaffe by bringing the horse to a better balance with increased impulsion, rather than pressing the brake and the accelerator pedal at the same time. The result will be at least honourable, even if the horse has only the potential of a small car.

Working in-hand

The old masters taught the piaffe in the pillars, which make either stepping back or going forward impossible for the horse. Since their use presents, therefore, many more disadvantages than advantages, one can understand why this method has fallen into disuse.

Because it allows complete freedom of movement, working in-hand has progressively substituted for the pillars – yet more proof, if it were needed, of the superiority of developing the piaffe with the help of transitions over all other methods of compression or restriction, however sophisticated.

Advantages

Not all horses have to be worked in-hand to learn the piaffe, but all improve with it, and some absolutely require it.

• Without the rider, the horse can balance himself more easily and find the right movement.
• The presence of the trainer at the horse's shoulder develops irreplaceable trust and closeness.
• Based on clear agreements and methodical work, the horse can begin to learn to collect very early – even before he has reached the level of education necessary to begin with the same work under the saddle. Anything that is done well is never premature, but always beneficial.

Principles

To obtain in-hand the quality of transitions necessary for the development of collection, the trainer must have the means to influence and control the three separate components of forward movement – tempo, posture and activity.

The work is introduced on the cavesson with side reins once the horse is confirmed on the lunge. Later, once the horse is correctly mise en main, one can continue the work in-hand on the curb with the reins held very short behind the chin groove.

First phase

The trainer teaches the horse to concentrate on him and follow him like a shadow. The horse must go absolutely straight along the walls on both reins.

Forwards

At the halt, the trainer stands by the horse's shoulder holding the lead rope about twenty centimetres from the cavesson and the whip horizontally alongside the hindquarters: if the trainer advances, the horse must follow immediately. If he delays or hesitates, he is encouraged to follow presently and quickly by the use of the whip associated with a voice aid. The trainer then praises the horse.

It is important to teach the horse to advance immediately and frankly at the walk or trot, without requiring either the whip or the voice.

Halts

From the walk or the trot, if the trainer slows or stops the horse must do the same. If this does not happen, or he tries to go on against the hand, the trainer first raises his hand in front of the horse's nose (a warning), then jerks the cavesson repeatedly, together with

Piaffe in the cavesson

Collection

Piaffe on the curb

the lumbar spine by repeated low touches with the whip. Bring the horse forward in trot and then praise. Appropriate adjustment of the side reins and the position of the hand guiding the cavesson determine the optimum posture of the forehand.

Piaffe while advancing
With fluid, energetic and close trot, rein-back, trot transitions, one obtains the shortening of the base of support and increased impulsion that are necessary to produce the piaffe, moving forwards at first, then in place.

During the piaffe repetitions, the trainer holds the whip vertically (as a visual cue) and uses a click of the tongue only as a last warning. Too many horses are dulled by uninterrupted, superfluous voice aids. The rider should also practise 'descente of the tongue!'

Do not use the whip to maintain action or to extend the piaffe, but only to correct laziness when taking the trot. Little by little the horse must be taught to begin to piaffe at the simple raising of the whip and some discreet voice aids should be enough to admonish him.

Use of the whip
First of all it is important that the horse does not fear the whip. He must be taught to accept its touch on his back and remain immobile. The whip must be used thoughtfully, because its effect depends on the 'touch point' selected and the muscle groups it animates.

Undesireable methods
Obtaining the piaffe through repeated taps on the croup is a harmful but widespread practice. This only provokes contractions of the gluteal and ischio-tiberal muscles which causes the horse to rear and not to lower the haunches. This, by the way, is how one produces the rearing required for the capriole.

Horses that have been taught to piaffe in this way do it by 'hopping' – that is, with their croup higher than the withers. This mobility of the hind legs is artificial and brings the horse on to

associated voice aids, until the halt is obtained. The trainer then praises the horse.

By repeating the exercise, the horse soon learns to halt from the walk, then from the trot, without the need for the trainer to intervene with the cavesson.

Rein-back
From the halt, if the trainer points the whip to the ground, places himself rearward of the shoulder and moves toward the rear, the horse should accompany him, no more and no less. If necessary, backing can be encouraged through the use of the cavesson (raising the hand, then jerking). Praise once the horse responds to the request to come forward once again without hesitation.

Transitions
At the end of this apprenticeship, the horse moves at the walk or trot, lengthens or shortens the gait, goes backward and comes forward again, all at the same time as the trainer, without having to resort to the whip or cavesson. The latter can then assume other roles.

Second phase
Once the horse reliably follows all the trainer's movements, it becomes possible to improve the rein-back and bring the trot, rein-back, trot transitions closer together to achieve the first piaffe-like steps.

Collecting the rein-back
While reining-back slowly, the trainer encourages engagement of the hind legs and flexion of

the forehand: a pseudo-piaffe, absolutely the opposite of what is desired. Vigorous use of the whip on the croup is only of real use to correct a horse that crushes its haunches by over-engaging the hind legs with an artificial rear. The old masters called this method 'tightening the garters'.

Using the whip on the cannons of the hind legs is also to be condemned, and not only because it is inelegant and harsh.

Lack of activity stems from a lack of impulsion and that can be only be corrected by forward movement. A trainer who thinks himself an expert as he bustles about like this with the whip fights against the effect and not the cause. He generates only tense, artificial movements that have no value.

In the end, such 'authoritarian' methods are unworthy of an écuyer, even if cleverly applied.

Useful methods

If the horse is prepared correctly and has the fundamentals well established (impulsion, balance), one can improve the movement by touching some carefully selected points.

• Insufficient flexion of the lumbar spine:
Touch with the whip on the origin of the tail. If the horse draws his tail in, he automatically increases the flexion in his lumbar spine and engagement of the hind legs – above all in rein-back but also in the piaffe.

• Insufficient flexion of the hind legs:
The trainer holds the whip horizontally and at right angles to the horse's body and touches each hind leg between hock and pastern at the moment of loading. This tapping on the front of the cannon-bones stimulates the muscles that flex the hocks and makes the movement springy.

• Insufficient height and flexion of the forelegs
This happens in particular if the horse stands over himself in front. In the first instance, raise the neck as far as possible, even if the angle at the poll must be clearly opened. This stretches the humero-mastoid muscles as they approach the vertical. In this posture the horse pulls his shoulders upwards and reestablishes his forelegs in a vertical position as he lightens his forehand.

With the horse in this posture, repeatedly touching the chest activates the humero-mastoid and pectoral muscles which bring the forelegs to the horizontal. Proceeding in this way, one activates the whole forehand of the horse who advances on the whip while elevating himself.

To be useful, these touches must produce very lively reactions which then continue with the barest hint of the whip. One must reward even the slightest anticipation, since the aim is merely to indicate with the whip and, in the end, to not need it at all.

Piaffe on long reins

Using long reins can make a valuable contribution to learning the piaffe if one follows some precautions, because the trainer is connected directly to the horse's mouth and takes up a

Long reins attached in the 'Mauleon' style

dangerous position in the blind spot of the horse's field of view. This assumes that the horse has been prepared with transitions in-hand, that he obeys voice aids on the lunge perfectly and, finally, that the trainer protects himself against the risk of kicking.

First phase

Repeat the work on transitions already established in-hand while placing oneself at an angle behind the croup, that is, within the horse's field of view but out of reach of a possible kick. The horse adjusts his movements to those of the trainer with help from the language of voice aids previously established. The piaffe is obtained from this position along the walls on both reins.

Second phase

Repeat the same work from a position behind the horse, in the horse's blind spot, but still out of reach of a kick. Attaching the reins to the

Piaffe on long reins in Münster

cavesson in the 'Mauleon' style enables the trainer to obtain a high degree of elevation and at the same channel the hindquarters with the reins while still remaining at a safe distance.

Third phase
Make sure that the horse does not kick out before continuing the work close behind him. Since an accident is always possible, even with the kindest horse, one must teach him beforehand that he may not do so under any circumstances.

Proceed as follows: have the horse piaffe along the wall near a corner and keep some distance away from his hind legs. Using the whip, ask for more and more until one provokes the beginning of an undesirable reaction. Reprimand immediately with the voice and a sharp lash of the whip on the thigh (do not punish on the croup). With his head in the corner, the horse must suffer this reprimand without being able to flee. Calm him again and then go forward to the shoulder to praise him. This lesson, repeated as often as necessary, quickly teaches the horse to piaffe extremely energetically while understanding that kicking out is absolutely prohibited.

This method may seem harsh, but it is the only one that leads to a degree of safety, which one can never take for granted, in any case. Work on long reins directly behind the horse always includes an element of risk and requires great care.

Piaffe under saddle

Observations about assistance from the ground
The idea of teaching a horse to begin or improve the piaffe with the active help of an 'assistant' with a whip is as dubious as it is widespread. In the first place, just as with misuse of the whip while working the horse in-hand, one can only achieve artificial effects, and not deal with causes. That much we have already covered. Secondly, one makes the serious mistake of underestimating the power of the horse's memory. He very quickly learns that he must exert himself so long as the 'supervisor' is nearby but that he can play up with impunity as soon as he goes away. One wouldn't do it any differently if one

wanted to teach him that the rider is completely insignificant. The more the rider accepts this kind of help from a 'coach', the more defenceless and powerless he becomes in the face of the horse's resistances when no one is there.

Many horses which have been 'trained' in the piaffe by this 'carpet-beater' method exact their revenge for this false conception and coarse abuse when it becomes time to 'perform'. They have my full sympathy!

Piaffe by transitions

Everything we have established concerning the work in-hand and on long reins also applies to work on the piaffe under the saddle, with or without any preparation on foot. By perfecting the transitions between trot and rein-back, the rider gradually brings the horse to the piaffe, in légèreté and without compression.

Achieving frank, fluid, close-order transitions requires that the rider build and refine a precise language of the aids. One may not mix or muddle the use of the aids in any way.
- Trot: upper body vertical, fingers open, legs active at the girth.
- Collecting the trot and halt: upper body taken back, fingers closed, legs active behind the girth.
- Rein-back: upper body leaning slightly forward, fingers closed, legs passive behind the girth or 'filtering'.
- Piaffe: upper body taken back, hand passive or 'filtering', legs active behind the girth.
- Trot: upper body returns to the vertical, fingers open, legs return to the girth.

In summary

By the posture of his upper body alone, the rider brings the horse in front of or behind himself. While moving forward, taking the shoulders back invites the horse to slow down. With his hands, the rider changes the posture of the head and neck according to his needs; filters the forward movement, elevates, slows down, stops or directs backward in harmony with his seat. With his legs the rider determines the desired degree of activity. Acting at the girth they send the horse forward. Gliding to the rear they approach the stomach muscles to provoke the engagement of the hind legs, flexion of the lumber spine and lowering of the haunches – now always in harmony with the seat during downwards transitions, rein-back or in the piaffe.

This valuable dynamic flexion of all joints of the hindquarters, from the hocks to the lumbar spine, can be supported by judicious use of the whip. As we have seen, using the whip on the croup causes the horse to hop and, hence, should be avoided. Repeated, concurrent touches of the haunches with two whips, on the other hand, provokes flexion of the lumbar spine, engages the hind legs and efficiently supports the aids of the legs while behind the girth – whether during downwards transitions, rein-back or in the piaffe.

Correcting irregular steps

If the horse produces asymmetrical steps in the piaffe, the cause is a lack of straightness and the associated tensions and balance disturbances. One can see that using the whip, however skilfully, does nothing to help because it tackles only the effects and not the cause – which, by the way, it very often aggravates.

Let's take the classic example of a horse with more activity in the right diagonal than the left in the piaffe. The phenomenon is linked to his natural left bend which brings with it a left hind leg that engages more than the right and a right

Piaffe on the snaffle

Piaffe on the curb in Münster

hind leg that pushes more than the left one. One corrects this asymmetry by de-contracting the horse and exercising the piaffe while in a right bend and in positions that compensate for the natural tendencies of the hind legs.

For example:

• Begin the piaffe after rein-back on a circle on the right rein, because the right side is considerably shortened and the right haunch must carry more weight.

• Piaffe while advancing in right shoulder-in position, because this makes the right hind engage more than the left while the left shoulder reaches further forward.

• Piaffe while advancing in 'head to the wall' to the right, because the left hind leg must push more strongly than the right one.

• Piaffe on a small circle on the right rein with the haunches in because, in addition to the preceding effects, one adds a reduction of the load on the left shoulder and an increased loading of the right haunch.

• Finally, the piaffe is improved in the pirouette.

All of these exercises, but especially those in the shoulder-in position, enable one to correct a horse with a tendency, as was the case with Odin, to piaffe by splaying his hind legs and standing over in front.

The passage

While collecting a gait, the horse gains in elevation what he loses in stride length. The passage is the extreme stylisation of the trot in which the horse realises the best possible compromise between horizontal propulsion and vertical projection.

In the passage, the horse springs from one diagonal leg pair to the other by maximum prolongation of the suspension phase and seems immune to the effects of gravity. In this way he expresses his full nobility.

Passage in the arena in Seville

The passage arises from a trot that becomes more cadenced because it is slowed without any loss of activity. Hence, work at the passage is best illustrated by the formula in Table 10.

As for the piaffe, it is by developing the quality and frequency of transitions that the trainer can, little by little, connect together the necessary elements – activity, balance and the appropriate tempo – that produce the passage. These transitions are basically performed within the trot, however:
• Impulsion – improves through frank, short, repeated increases in the trot.
• Balance – checked by repeated, easy shortening of the trot.

As these transitions become more frank and more fluid, the rider can bring them closer and closer together, marrying their effects by transference and not by compression. There comes a time when the horse, always ready to spring forward, shortens the gait without loss of activity and begins to suspend himself in the 'doux passage' ('gentle' passage) as the old masters called it.

Clear differentiation of the aids allows the horse to recognise the passage properly and to understand the rider's wishes. Bit by bit, the latter can reduce the preparation time and extend and improve the periods of passage itself.

• Lengthening the trot: upper body vertical, fingers open, legs active at the girth.
• Shortening the trot and asking for passage: the rider stretches up, takes the shoulders back, lifts the hand, the legs act behind the girth to animate the horse in the rhythm of the gait.

The transitions are varied according to the natural balance and temperament of the horse:
• With a cold, lazy horse one asks for frequent, frank and very energetic lengthening. Send the horse energetically forwards at the slightest sign of a reduction in the passage – do not try to maintain the passage with spurs or a whip. Reward the going forwards.
• With a hot-blooded horse the accent is put on slowing down; stop and rein-back as often as necessary. Begin the passage again in an appropriate balance. Halt. Reward immobility.

Whether in-hand, on long reins or under saddle, the passage originates from the interplay of the transitions at the trot.

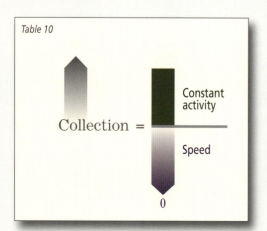

Collection

Correction of irregularities

As in the piaffe, possible irregularities in the passage arise from a lack of straightness and balance due to natural asymmetry. If we again examine the case of a horse naturally bent to the left, one proceeds as with the piaffe:
- De-contract and bend to the right.
- Passage on the circle on the right hand.
- Passage in right shoulder-in position.
- Passage in travers on the right rein.
- Passage in travers on the circle on the right rein.

Conclusions

If we take up our motoring metaphor again, the passage corresponds to the problem of slowing down. There are two possibilities:
- The driver is going fast, remains in the same gear and slows down with the brakes. The speed drops rapidly, and in the extreme case the engine dies when he tries to accelerate again. This is the style of a Sunday driver.
- The driver doesn't touch the brakes. He reduces speed by changing down through the gears and taking advantage of engine braking. The decrease in road speed goes hand in hand with the increase in engine speed. This enables him to accelerate again immediately with full power. This is an efficient style of driving that spares the brakes, the style of a 'racing' driver.

The transition to passage can be compared to this decrease in speed achieved thanks to the power of the engine rather than by braking.

Priorities and transitions

The question often arises whether one should teach the piaffe or the passage first. This, of course, depends on the horse.

As spectacular as it may be, the passage is, if one takes a closer look, a substantially less collected gait than is generally thought. In the passage the horse pushes off forwards and upwards. It gains in elevation what it loses in stride length. This assumes that the horse relieves his forehand, transfers weight to the haunches and increases the flexion of the joints of the limbs – but does not at all require him to flex his lumbar spine and lower his haunches. In the passage the horse shortens his steps but not his base of support. In the very spectacular 'grand passage' the horse often shows an inclination to lengthen his base of support towards the rear!

These facts explain why horses that are naturally endowed with an energetic, cadenced trot can reach the passage so easily and so early. One can say that their trot already contains the passage at its core. One must always use it with a little skill.

From this one can draw the following conclusions:
- The passage is closely connected to the aptitudes of the horse, while the piaffe depends above all on the skill of the rider.
- A horse which has first learned the piaffe derives the passage from it bit by bit and transitions from piaffe to passage without any major difficulties – since he goes from greater to lesser collection. On the other hand, a horse that learned the passage first on account of an advantageous trot will encounter all kinds of trouble in deriving the piaffe from it, because he must also increase his degree of collection. Shortening the passage carries a double risk of seeing the horse allow the passage to 'die' or attempt a 'passagey' piaffe. All in all, this theoretically enticing approach turns out to be catastrophic in practice. The chance of correct transitions is minimal.
- The transition from passage to piaffe is by far the most difficult one. Without changing the cadence, the horse must shorten the passage steps by flexing his lumbar spine and engaging his hind legs until he piaffes.
- Since a good piaffe is the essence of collection and the foundation of everything, one absolutely must start with piaffe with horses that have a moderate trot. It enables them to develop expression and cadence and then derive the passage from it.

In the arena at Nîmes

- With a horse that has an advantageous trot and comes easily to the passage, the rider must watch out not to indulge himself in it and must work separately and simultaneously on the piaffe.

One can conclude the exploration of this question with two points:
- The ideal is, as General Decarpentry advises, to progress both airs at the same time so that, afterwards, one can connect them correctly.
- Under these conditions, not only can one consider the transitions to be on a sound basis, they will even contribute to the improvement of the two airs by making the piaffe more active and the passage more balanced. Once more it is clear that transitions contribute more to the development of an air than just working on it by itself.

The pesade

'One makes use of this air to teach the horse to raise his forehand lightly with gracefully folded forelegs and to strengthen him on his hindquarters.' *(La Guérinière)*

The pesade is the culmination of collection, corresponding to the complete mastery of balance.

To achieve it, the horse must above all have a very good piaffe, then be capable of engaging his hind legs so far under his body and shortening his base of support so much that he can lift his forelegs off the ground and pause for a few moments in balance on lowered haunches. This air is the exact opposite of rearing, the horse standing straight up on his hindquarters.

In consideration of the effort and the degree of balance that the pesade requires, one must teach it from the ground at first. Whether this air is requested in-hand, on long reins or under saddle – preparation, precautions and corrections are based on the same principles:

Pesade on the cavesson

- Introduce a clear differentiation between the aids for the 'ordinary' piaffe and the piaffe with increased engagement that serves as a preparation for the pesade. This is indispensable if the rider wants to avoid the horse first of all becoming confused or in the end, offering the pesade unsolicited.

- The academic piaffe is performed in place and in a posture of maximum elevation. To avoid any misunderstanding and to guarantee impulsion and roundness, one should always ask for the 'pesade-piaffe' in forward motion and with a lower posture.

While working on the pesade:
• If the horse anticipates the aids, send him energetically forwards at the slightest sign of hanging back.
• If he appears lazy, restore an energetic piaffe before asking for the pesade once more.
• If he drops heavily back onto his forehand, back him up, begin the piaffe again and ask once more.
• Always finish the session with the piaffe without asking for the pesade.

Pesade on the curb

Pesade in-hand

The initial phase is conducted on the snaffle with cavesson and side reins.
• Beginning with an energetic piaffe, ask for the over-engagement while moving forward via low touches with the whip.
• When the horse appears ready, ask him to elevate using the cavesson hand while opposing any backward movement of the hocks with the whip.

• If necessary, an assistant can act with a whip on the horse's chest to encourage him to fold his forelegs correctly.

The most important thing is not that the horse maintains the pesade for a long time, especially in the beginning, but that he raises and lowers himself into and out of the air with graceful slowness while remaining de-contracted and round. With progressive practice, the horse will gain in confidence as well as strengthening his hindquarters and the duration of the pesade can be extended little by little, within the limits of his capacity.

• Once confirmed, the pesade can be performed on the curb. In this case the reins are adjusted and held crossed in one hand placed behind the withers. This assumes, of course, that the horse is correctly 'mis en main'.

Pesade on long reins

If the horse is confirmed in the piaffe on long reins and has already learned the pesade in-hand, one can begin to practise this air also on long reins. In the first phase the trainer pays attention to safety, remaining behind the horse at an angle and staying in his field of view. In the second phase he can step behind the horse and repeat the work previously completed.

Ask for the piaffe with increased engagement with voice aids and low touches of the whip. When the horse is sufficiently on the haunches, elevate him by the use of the hands while opposing any attempt to step back with the whip. Send the horse energetically forward any time his hocks so much as begin to step back even slightly. Begin again with the piaffe and ask for the pesade once more.

Ground rules

If the trainer is standing behind his horse, he must have in place some precise signals that avoid any misunderstandings on the part of the horse.

Verdi in May 1998, pesade in a sparkling shower of pollen.

- Normal piaffe: the lines are held high either side of the hindquarters.
- 'Pesade-piaffe': the lines are held lower down along either side of the hindquarters, enveloping and, therefore, activating them at thigh level.

To refresh the horse's memory, one should also frequently practise from the lateral position.

Pesade under saddle

Once a horse has learned the pesade with the trainer on the ground, one can progress to performing it under saddle.

Proceed as follows:
- To avoid any confusion with the normal piaffe, the rider asks for the piaffe that prepares for the pesade by taking his legs back a little further. To be consistent, the greater the desired response, the more the legs should approach the belly. By intensifying the alternating touches of the legs, the rider brings the hind legs further and further under the mass, but always advancing a little to prevent the horse anticipating the exercise.
- When the rider feels that the haunches are very low and the forehand is light, he fixes the horse's hind legs by closing both of his legs (supported by the spurs if necessary) and asks the horse to lift his forehand from the ground by taking his upper body back and raising his hand. The rider, therefore, asks the horse to balance himself with the greatest possible weight transfer onto the hindquarters while his legs prevent any backwards movement. In order to avoid disturbing the very sensitive balance of the pesade, the rider keeps his upper body perpendicular to the ground.

The pesade is more successful the more slowly and more gracefully the horse begins and leaves it, maintaining it with the aids en descente. Its duration will depend on the horse's level of experience and, above all, on the power of his hindquarters.

Observations

The usefulness of the pesade lies in the fact that this air is the touchstone of collection. In fact, one cannot consider it without a very good piaffe and it requires an extremely unstable balance that cannot be forced or faked through tricks. This air, which requires trust, suppleness, balance and strength, cannot be achieved through the application of force. Quite rightly it was highly regarded by the old masters and considered the foundation of all the school leaps.

How can it be that an air of such technical interest and aesthetic value – painters and sculptors never miss it – has disappeared from French riding? By which process have we gone from the pesade (the horse calmly stabilised on his haunches) to the courbette (the horse briefly standing on his hind legs)? In response, one can identify three points:

• In the French Revolution, the academies disappeared, and with them almost all of the skills and experience in this domain.
• The 'dandyism' of the nineteenth century, with its predilection for the 'sports horse' and disdain for the 'school horse', gradually called time on practices that were judged outdated and superfluous.
• 'Once the Art was exiled from Versailles… There remained only the École de Saumur in which it could be preserved …'.

This intention originates from the Comte d'Aure, écuyer at the School of Versailles up to its final closing in 1830, then écuyer en chef at Saumur from 1847 to 1855. But the imperatives of military riding instruction, with its natural penchant for manoeuvres in 'close order' ranks, soon turned out to be incompatible with certain lessons. Highly demanding, the pesade is something for the individual écuyer – but now ten riders must execute the air on command at the same time with horses 'trained' accordingly. This new movement has been passed down to us under the incorrect name 'courbette'. The likely origin of this semantic divergence came from the pen of the first écuyer en chef, J. B. Cordier who wrote in his Traité raisonné d'équitation in 1824: 'From the pesade or courbette in place.'

Odin in Saumur 1986

This is how some traditions disappear and others are born. In this case a subtle, discreet air disappeared in favour of something military and spectacular. Comte d'Aure judged as follows: 'In militarising even the écuyers of the School, in becoming a military stepping board, the Art could only suffer, and this is what has happened.'

This explains, anyway, why nowadays a trainer who is interested in the pesade is thought of as eccentric and regarded as an archaeologist.

Canter pirouettes

In principle, the pirouette is a pure rotation of the forehand around the haunches. Bent throughout his body, the horse pivots on his inside hind leg, which steps on the same spot again and again. The pirouette requires a travers position (which facilitates the extreme crossing of the forelegs) as well as a degree of collection appropriate to the movement (transfer of weight to the hindquarters, in particular the inside hind leg thus relieving the forehand and enabling it to move).

At the walk, the pirouette requires good collection. At the trot, it requires that the horse piaffes. At the canter the pirouette forces a degree of collection that corresponds logically to the canter in place.

Canter pirouette to the right in Münster

Canter pirouette to the left

Preparation of the canter pirouette

The rider must connect the travers position with a degree of collection that leads almost to the canter in place.

Collect the canter in travers position

In travers on the circle, develop the walk-canter transition. The transitions are brought gradually closer together, then performed on smaller circles while always maintaining the travers (haunches-in) position.

Collect and bend the horse while maintaining the straightness of the canter.

• On a single track on the circle: repeat close-coupled transitions between rein-back and canter:
Collected canter → walk → halt → rein-back on the circle → collected canter, etc.
Collected canter → halt → rein-back → canter → halt → rein-back → canter, etc.
• On a straight line, in a slight shoulder-in position (shoulder-fore):
Collected canter → halt → collected canter → working canter → collected canter → halt → collected canter, etc.

Notes

With a horse that is naturally bent to the left, one must take special care in transitions in travers position on the right rein as well as with shoulder-fore at the canter on the left rein. In the course of these transitions, the horse must be happy to progressively shorten the canter without losing activity, ready to 'sit down' or go forward at any moment, while remaining incurved throughout.

Progression of pirouettes

The 'Baroque volte': the horse describes a square with a quarter pirouette in each corner.
• On two tracks: ride in travers position on the sides with a quarter pirouette in every corner.
• On a single track: slight shoulder-fore on the sides. Quarter pirouette in the corners.

This work is begun on a large square which leaves enough space to send the horse forwards again after every quarter pirouette and then collect the canter to negotiate the next corner. As the horse develops his ability to maintain collection, the rider can reduce the size of the square and thus bring the quarter pirouettes closer together.

Preparation of canter pirouettes on various figures

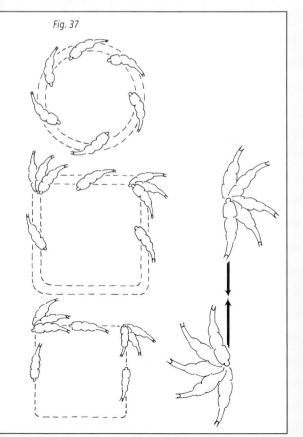

Fig. 37

The passade

A sequence of half-pirouettes connected by riding back and forth on the same straight line. At first, one keeps the half-pirouettes well apart to allow the necessary time for preparation. Once the horse remains collected and straight, one can bring them closer together.

The pirouette

A horse that can perform a series of correct passades should have little difficulty in performing a whole pirouette, repeating them or even doubling them. Any time the horse hesitates or makes a mistake, return to the half-pirouette or the work on the Baroque volte.

Canter pirouette to the right on long reins

Encounters

I had the opportunity to meet Nuno Oliveira on three occasions, two of them at the School. On his last visit to Saumur I was able to present Odin in front of him. He observed his work very carefully and, it seemed to me, with interest. He made very few comments but from his questions I understood how much it moved him to see a Portuguese horse under the saddle of an écuyer of the Cadre Noir and at the forefront of presentations of this institution.

Some years later, a long time after Nuno Oliveira's death, Antoine de Coux who had been close to him for a long time, told me all the good things he had said to him about Odin's work. I was inclined to take him at his word, because the man was not known for flattery, and there was no way of knowing that we would meet one day.

But not all meetings leave good memories. For one week in autumn, 1989, the School hosted the international dressage rider and coach of the Soviet team, Ivan Kalita, with full honours.

One morning in the Manège des écuyers, after I had just warmed Odin up a little, I asked Mr Kalita, via his translator, whether he would do me the honour of riding my horse. Barely in the saddle, he put him into a strong trot and spent ten minutes making him perform transitions like crazy, alternating between abrupt attacks with the spurs and barely gentler demi-arrêts. After that he dismounted, left the horse where he was and turned his heels without saying a word. A little taken aback, I asked him nevertheless for his opinion of the horse. Without giving me so much as a glance, he replied to the translator who passed on the champion's judgment to me: 'Doesn't go forward, not on the aids ...'

Staggered more by his coarse behaviour than his dry judgment, I was dumbfounded for a few moments, then furious. Everything has its limits,

Face to face: Odin with Monsieur Humeau, his favourite groom

the caprices of a dressage diva just as much as the obligations of the host; I decided to protest with the deference due to such a special guest. So, I remounted my horse and began riding ostentatiously on a large circle around this man planted in the middle of the manège. I spared him nothing: canter pirouettes, passage, piaffe, pesades and Spanish walk. Although he endured the show with the perfect indifference of someone who has seen it all before, I left the hall convinced of having made my point.

This unfortunate tale reveals some behaviour which is not so very rare and suggests to me every time the same thoughts. Mainly, that 'dressage rider', 'écuyer' and 'man of honour' are not necessarily the same thing, while also recalling the saying: 'I have experienced all forms of depravity, including fame.'

In April 1995, the Cadre Noir appeared in Münster, a stronghold of German riding where we were received very well. One of the gala evenings took place under the chairmanship of Dr. Reiner Klimke, a man who needs no introduction. Colonel Carde and five or six écuyers, of whom I was one, had the honour of being invited to a dinner with him. Sometime between main course and dessert, the écuyer en chef asked Herr Klimke whether he would like to give his impressions of the performance and to inform us what he had liked best of all. Our host answered politely that he had very much appreciated all of our presentations; however, he had particularly liked the grey stallion. Of those there was only one and I knew him rather well – and for a little while I almost forgot the insults of 'Ivan the terrible'!

After each gala performance, a part of the audience is granted access behind the scenes and comes to visit the horses. One evening a lady of a certain age stood in front of Odin's box. When I approached her, she asked me:
'Monsieur, is this the horse who was in the long reins?'
'Yes, Madame ...'
'Ah, Monsieur, please forgive me, I know nothing about it – but it was unbelievable, it was as if the horse was all alone!'
'Please, don't apologise', I answered, 'that is exactly the goal we aim for – and without doubt the nicest compliment which I have ever received!'

Experts sometimes maintain a certain condescending disdain for the opinion of the layman and, in so doing, they are often the ones who miss the real point.

Half-pass to the right in trot on long reins in Münster

The Spanish walk

'French equitation of the last century contains some valuable gymnastic exercises, like the Spanish walk and Spanish trot, which the German critics of the time and today's so-called purists call artificial gaits.' *(Nuno Oliveira)*

Spanish walk is a slow, cadenced walk that the horse performs with sustained elevation and extension of the forelegs. It has an aesthetic value and gymnastic usefulness only under certain conditions:
• The horse must remain perfectly in ramener, with impeccable fixity of the head, progressing energetically with the back and haunches, instead of nodding at every step.
• In addition, his movements must be symmetrical, with long strides, while maintaining a regular, four-beat rhythm. The movements should be rounded and reach well out in front. The horse must neither 'waddle' nor 'beat the dust'.
• Finally, the horse must remain straight, without swaying in the shoulders or putting his hindquarters at an angle.

Jambette at the halt

Single jambette in forward motion

Spanish walk in-hand

Spanish walk going forward from the touch with the whip on the chest

Preparation

Even if executed perfectly, one must admit that the Spanish walk brings the shoulders of the horse more into play than the hindquarters. Hence, introducing it prematurely carries the risk of raising the head and neck with a hollow back, above all if the horse is built downhill and lacks energy.

Therefore, one should not start it before the horse has a good piaffe. If this condition is met, the Spanish walk is a gymnastic exercise without equal for horses with tight shoulders and forelegs that stand behind the vertical.

Jambettes

Working from the ground

At the halt along the long side of the arena, the jambette is requested by tapping on the inside foreleg with the whip. Reward the slightest raising of the leg, even if it is in reaction to an irritation. The movement increases with repetition. Generally one obtains more elevation of the leg by touching between the knee and the chest, more extension by touching between the knee and the fetlock.

As soon as the jambette starts to appear, one connects with it the raising of the snaffle rein on the same side and then introduces forwards movement. If the horse has been worked correctly in-hand, the rider must only advance in order that the horse follows him. Bit by bit, the rider can dispense with the aids from the whip, except as a reminder of the jambette.

At this stage, the rider can ask for jambettes while advancing and, therefore, repeat them and hence bring them closer and closer together – until it occurs with every step of the inside foreleg. The rider must pay attention to achieving equally good quality of movements on both reins.

Once the jambettes are confirmed on both reins, one must begin to request jambettes from

Spanish walk during a presentation at the National School of Equitation

the outside foreleg, first at the halt, then in motion. Once beyond this stage, the rider can ask for two successive jambettes, then three, four, five steps of Spanish walk, raising the inside and outside rein alternately. Repeat the same work on both reins.

The final stage, perhaps leading to perfection: ask for the Spanish walk while holding the curb reins behind the chin groove and tapping with the whip on the chest. This activates the whole forehand and reminds the horse to advance on the tap of the whip, producing an energetic and brilliant Spanish walk. Timid or lazy horses can be improved in this manner.

Work under saddle

The progression followed in-hand is repeated under saddle. The rider asks for a jambette at the halt by elevation and the indirect rein, possibly supported by touches with the whip which is held in the same hand along the shoulder. The next stage consists of obtaining closer and closer successive jambettes while advancing. This leads to jambettes of the inside foreleg at every step. Repeat the work carefully on each rein. Then in the last phase of preparation, the rider focuses on obtaining jambettes with the outside foreleg at every step, on both reins.

If these conditions are fulfilled, the rider can eventually obtain two then three, four, five steps of jambettes one after the other and thus form a complete sequence of the Spanish walk. With the perfection of the air, the use of the whip becomes increasingly rare until the seat and legs become sufficient to cadence the gait alongside discreetly alternating indirect reins.

'This is an extremely useful exercise: it produces enormous development of the shoulders and extends the range of movement of the forelegs. In connection with the gymnastics that one applies to the hindquarters, it makes the horse mobile, elastic and brilliant.' *(Nuno Oliveira)*

Ridden in close-order transitions with the collected trot, the Spanish walk allows the rider to bring every horse – even the most modest – to the passage. If we add that it undeniably promotes the rider's tact, we can conclude that it is always a pity when it is cast aside.

Spanish walk in front of the château de Saumur

The Spanish walk

157

The future

When I took my leave from the École Nationale d'Équitation, I obtained assurances from the management that, because of his age, Odin would be retired as soon as possible, after what was then thirteen years' loyal service of rare intensity.

In fact, however, he was discharged a year later, in July 1999, without having been used in any further presentations. I got him back lame and in a miserable physical and mental state. At least he was cheap!

General de Gaulle once said: 'Old age is a shipwreck.' I have two goals: to spare this horse a mediocre end and guarantee him a comfortable old age.

Whatever may happen, the purpose of this book is to pay homage to an exceptional partner and to pass him on to future generations – since only what one forgets dies completely.

'He was a little white horse
All behind, all behind,
He is a little white horse,
All behind and him in front.'
(Paul Fort)

Hanover, May 2000

Epilogue

After two years in Germany, Odin returned to France. He has covered a few mares and sired ten foals. Since 2003 he has been enjoying his old age in the département d'Isère with one of my oldest friends, Jacky La Corte. He is looking forward cheerfully to his 29th birthday.

May 2008